MW00986683

Church and Academy
in Harmony

Church and Academy
in Harmony

Models of Collaboration for the Twenty-First Century

ANTHONY L. BLAIR

PICKWICK *Publications* · Eugene, Oregon

CHURCH AND ACADEMY IN HARMONY
Models of Collaboration for the Twenty-First Century

Pickwick Publications
An Imprint of Wipf and Stock Publishers
199 W. 8th Ave., Suite 3
Eugene, OR 97401

www.wipfandstock.com

ISBN 13: 978-1-60899-507-3

Cataloging-in-Publication data:

Blair, Anthony L.

Church and academy in harmony : models of collaboration for the twenty-
first century / Anthony L. Blair.

viii + 126 p. ; 21 cm. —Includes bibliographical references and index.

ISBN 13: 978-1-60899-507-3

1. Church and education. 2. Universities and colleges—Religion. I. Title.

BV1610.B53 2010

Manufactured in the U.S.A.

Contents

Tables

Acknowledgments

"If I have seen further than others, it is because I have stood on the shoulders of giants." While I know full well that one or more giants have occasionally hoisted me onto their shoulders, I am not ready to claim that I have seen or do see further than others. Indeed, I suspect that many of my mutterings are those of a blind man banging into furniture in an overcrowded room. Therefore, perhaps it would be best to simply say that if I have seen anything at all, it is because I have borrowed the eyeglasses of others.

"Nay, fair little stranger," said he, "I like not thy name and fain would I have it otherwise. Little art thou indeed, and small of bone and sinew, therefore shalt thou be christened Little John." Thus said Will Stutely to the man formerly known as John Little, according to one version of the Robin Hood legend. It is a presumptuous thing to bestow a name upon another human being. But it is another and better thing entirely to name those to whom debts are owed. I thus name the following individuals as some of those who have graciously lent me their glasses, telescopes, and microscopes and have invited me to glimpse what they see clearly, to add color to my monochromatic visions, to look in the dark spaces for treasure, to open the blinds and let the light invade the room. I am grateful to . . .

. . . my church, and by this I mean both my "tribe" (The Church of the United Brethren in Christ) and my local congregation (Hosanna! A Fellowship of Christians) . . .

... my academy, and by this I mean both my employer (Eastern University) and the institution in which these ideas were originally germinated (George Fox Evangelical Seminary) ...

... Leonard Sweet. Like Jesus, Len drives me crazy. And in much the same way ...

... Robin Baker, President of George Fox University, for his "spot on" review of earlier drafts of this work.

"My faith looks up to thee." If this little book changes even slightly the direction of a reader's vision, may it be upward. "Let us fix our eyes on Jesus, the author and finisher of our faith."

Anthony L. (Tony) Blair
Lititz, Pennsylvania
Spring 2010

1

Church and Academy on Pilgrimage

WALKING THE WAY OF TENSION

Spring, 2008

"You've got mail," chirped the annoying voice on Tim Herndon's laptop as he logged on. It required considerable discipline on his part to check his email every day he was in the office. He still preferred to pick up the phone and have a simple conversation. The phone was still his primary mode of communication with a number of members of his elder board, but he had reluctantly come to the conclusion that he was going to remain out of touch with many in his congregation if he did not accommodate himself to electronic communication. Scrolling down through his inbox, he was momentarily angered again as he noted how many advertisements slipped past his filters. But then he stopped. Just below a message from Nigeria asking him to accept millions of dollars in exchange for a bank account number and just above a message offering him the opportunity to meet young women in eastern Europe, he saw a message from Maria.

"Dear Pastor Tim," the message began, "I'm sorry to bother you, but I'm so confused. I did what you suggested and scheduled a personal interview with the chair of the Sociology Department at

Western Christian College. Dr. Fredericks is *so* smart, Pastor Tim! She listened to me carefully and answered my questions and got me so excited about going to school there. She seemed to really understand me, Pastor Tim! You know how important that is to me. Mom and Dad still don't get it. You've helped me see that I really can make a difference in the world, but I feel so unprepared. I think Dr. Fredericks can help me. She seems to believe in me . . . and she just met me!"

"What's the problem?" Tim wondered. "This sounds good." But Maria's next lines explained it. "But Dr. Fredericks doesn't seem to like our church very much. She talked pretty negatively about churches in general, particularly those in our denomination. I'm sure she loves Jesus—she even has a picture of him in her office and she has a Bible on her desk. But she kept talking about how close-minded her students are when they first come to college and how they leave her classrooms with a 'broader faith.' What does that mean, Pastor Tim? I thought this college was part of our denomination. Why would she be so negative about it?"

"Why, indeed?" Tim mused. But he wasn't overly surprised. This had happened before. Two years ago he had recommended the school to Jimmy Long, who was thinking about a career in youth ministry. Jimmy's parents had pulled him from the school in the middle of the first semester, after a chapel speaker had talked about historical errors in the Bible. And Jimmy said "everyone knew" that one of the professors was living a gay lifestyle. After leaving Western, Jimmy tried a semester in a fundamentalist Bible college, which didn't work very well for him either. They didn't approve of his music or his hair. The shame of it all was that Jimmy was now working in an optical shop, ostensibly to save money to go back to school. But Tim doubted that he would. Jimmy seemed increasingly unenthusiastic about the church and even the youth group.

"Well, we're not going to repeat that pattern," Tim vowed. He wrote a short message back to Maria. All his email replies were short, because he used the two-finger approach to typing. Besides, this wasn't an email matter. He invited her to visit him in his study sometime during the next week. In the meantime, he had another phone call or two to make.

Meanwhile, Barbara Fredericks walked down the hall to her office with a heavy heart. She had a policy of returning all student assignments to them at the very next class period, and that meant that she had twenty three-page papers to read and grade before the three o'clock class if she was going to maintain her policy. And the search committee was meeting at noon. But Barbara seldom failed to follow through. It was one of the reasons that the dean had asked her to chair the department last year, despite the fact she hadn't even been there long enough to qualify for tenure. But she wasn't too worried about that. She was proud of her accomplishment as the first African-American women to chair an academic department at Western Christian. Her teaching evaluations were good. She had won a major grant for the department just last Fall and her dissertation was soon to be published by a major academic press.

But now she had to deal with another distraction. A minister in the school's supporting denomination had called the dean's office complaining about her conversation with a prospective student. She didn't think it would hurt her relationship with the dean; he understood better than most how touchy many of the ministers were. But it was the kind of thing that gave headaches to President Hodge, and she didn't relish the possibility that he would hear about this. It seemed that these days he was constantly on the defensive at meetings of the board of trustees regarding denominational concerns about the college. She was sympathetic to his situation; it wasn't easy to explain to these people that the mission of the university was not merely to reinforce what was taught in the churches. The mission of the university was to teach students to *think*. And teaching them to think meant that they had to look at and understand various points of view. Ministers and parents didn't always understand that.

Barbara's spiritual roots were not in the denomination with which the college was affiliated. In fact, she didn't personally know any faculty members who were in that denomination, although she was sure that there had to be some on campus somewhere. She was raised in an African-American Pentecostal congregation, and still enjoyed visiting there when she went home to see family, but worshipped regularly now in an Episcopal church near campus, along with a number of her colleagues. It was a multiracial congregation with a well-educated priest, a beautiful old stone sanctuary with stained glass windows, and a liturgy that evoked history and mystery. The parishioners were largely upper middle class professionals, socially and politically liberal, and broad-minded in their theological commitments.

She enjoyed the atmosphere very much. Her faith had changed much in the years since she left home, but it had deepened. Her passion for Jesus was obvious on her face, or so her friends told her. He had *saved* her. She knew that. She knew what her life could have been, but God had drawn her out and given her a life mission and had gifted her to fulfill it. She loved Him so much.

She had worshipped once in one of the churches of the sponsoring denomination, perhaps even the church from which the pastor had just called to complain about her. She had been invited to speak to a Sunday School class (an outdated institution, she thought) at a suburban congregation on the subject of women in leadership. When she showed up, they seemed surprised that she was black. There were no other blacks in the congregation, as far as she could see. She had stayed for worship, which had been rather bland—a lot of worship choruses projected on a screen. They were good people. They treated her well. But she was uncomfortable nonetheless—with the American flag on the platform, with the undertones of biblical literalism, with the emphasis on personal salvation to the exclusion of social justice, with the seeming blindness and deafness to the real world of pain and suffering. They prayed for various congregational members with physical ailments but there were no prayers for unity among believers, for an end to oppression, for the hurting people in their own community. Their myopic vision was disheartening.

For his part, Tim hung up the phone feeling discouraged. His conversation with the dean, whom he knew from his days as a student 25 years ago, had gone about as expected. Dean Pierson had remembered him. He had been a young professor when Tim was a student at Western, and had made the study of history, which Tim had always considered a rather boring subject, really come alive. Tim wished he could teach with that level of energy and creativity. He was a tolerable preacher, he thought, but always seemed to get flummoxed in the give-and-take of a classroom setting. He always felt more comfortable when he was doing the talking and the audience was doing the listening. In any case, Tim and Dean Pierson had chatted a few times over the years, most recently during the "Jimmy episode."

Dean Pierson had been polite and even sympathetic when Tim called. But he was fairly adamant in his defense of Barbara Fredericks. "She's one of the best we have, Tim," he said. "And she's got a point. We get so many students in here who think that the purpose of a Christian university is merely to give them in-depth Bible studies or teach them apologetics or to explain why everyone else is wrong. That's not what we're about. This isn't youth group, Tim. It's higher education."

"I understand that, Dean Pierson," Tim countered. "All I'm asking is that your faculty members not destroy the faith of the Christian students we send there or I'm going to stop sending them. If I wanted their faith destroyed, I'd send them to the state university down the road. They're much cheaper and at least you know what you're getting there. But when I send one of my teens to Western, all of us—the student, their parents, and the church— believe that the college was founded to support the church. You can teach Maria Alvarez things we can never teach her, but you also have a responsibility for her soul. When she attends class at a Christian university and finds that some of her professors think that much that we've been teaching her is wrong, she'll begin to doubt her church, and her faith, and maybe even God. I know. That's already happened to one of my kids."

"Now don't blame what happened with Jimmy Long entirely on us," Dean Pierson countered gently. "He hurt himself by not attending classes. Remember? He thought his time was better spent in Bible study. And when he was in class, he was disruptive—always challenging the instructor. Jimmy had his mind made up before he got here. He wasn't exactly teachable."

Tim sighed. This wasn't getting anywhere. Yes, Jimmy wasn't the ideal college student type, but Maria was. Or could be, if they could just figure out what role college was supposed to play in her life. It was obvious that he had one vision for what the university was to be and Dean Pierson and Dr. Fredericks, and probably all of their colleagues, had another. Tim didn't consider himself close-minded—far from it. He read a lot, including viewpoints with which he didn't agree. But he knew that the main purpose of the church on this earth was to glorify God by saving souls. Anything that did not support that mission was of little long-term interest to him. When he was in college, the professors seemed to agree with that perspective. But that wasn't true anymore.

He thanked Dean Pierson for the phone conversation, hung up, and thought for a moment. He then made two additional calls. The first was to buzz his secretary in the next room to ask her to call several other Christian colleges with which he was somewhat familiar and ask them to send catalogs. He had to do some research. The second was his district superintendent, Carl Adams. It broke his heart to do so, but at the next district meeting, Tim wanted to present a motion that the denomination withdraw from its relationship with Western Christian. He knew that there would be opposition, but it would be opposition arising largely from nostalgia—from alumni like himself who remembered a time when the church and the university were working in tandem. But things had changed. And he suspected that Carl would agree.

Barbara Fredericks attended the search committee meeting at noon, where she argued passionately for a candidate with a degree from Yale and a track record of published scholarship. "How often does a little Christian school like Western get to consider such a high-quality candidate?" she questioned. This was a real opportunity to improve the reputation of her department and raise the academic profile of the college. The candidate's faith statement (a mandatory part of the application process) was a bit more liberal, theologically speaking, than what most of the other committees were comfortable with, but Barbara pressed the argument that theirs was an ecumenical Christian community of faith. They would only profit from another Christian perspective in their midst. As long as the candidate could sign the confession of faith—and she said she could—it was not in their best interest to reject her. Barbara had prevailed. An interview with the Yale candidate would be scheduled for two weeks from today.

After class, at which she returned assignments fully graded, and engaged her students in a stimulating discussion of the structural roots of racial injustice, she returned to her office. Picking up the phone, she called Ron Bettersby in the Religion Department. Last Fall Ron had circulated a petition among the faculty asking them to endorse a proposal to the board of trustees that the university rethink its relationship with the founding denomination. Barbara had not thought it a fight worth picking. She had known that the proposal, whether approved by the board or not, would result in ill will and a decrease in financial support. And if faculty salaries were ever going to be competitive, that financial support was certainly needed. Besides, she knew that Ron's proposal was motivated by his experience as the target of a witch-hunt by a few vocal denominational leaders because of his views on biblical inerrancy. While she was sympathetic to Ron, she hadn't been interested in fighting someone else's personal battle.

But today she had changed her mind. The relationship with the denomination was clearly more distraction than help. Better to go independent and be free to pursue God's truth wherever it was to be found than to work under the growing pressure of well-meaning but narrow-minded ministers like the one who had called her dean. The university needed a broader identity, a wider base of support, and a fresh commitment to academic freedom. "Ron?" she asked, "How can I get my name on your petition?"

Spring, 2010

Torn between her admiration for Pastor Tim and Dr. Fredericks, and dependent on her parents for her tuition, Maria eventually decided to keep things simple and cheap. She enrolled in the state university and commuted from home. During her second semester, she switched her major from sociology to accounting. She graduated last Spring and now works in accounts receivable at a local furniture factory. She's getting married in August to Jimmy Long, who's now managing the optical shop. They attend church once in a while.

A proposal to sever the relationship between what is now Western Christian University and its sponsoring denomination failed by a vote of 17 to 15 in 2009. Pastor Tim, now the district superintendent, and Barbara Fredericks, now the youngest dean in Western's history after Dean Pierson's retirement last Summer, are both mounting campaigns to try again next year. They have still never met.

WALKING THE WAY OF TRANSITION

The purpose of this book is to explore the growing tensions between church and academy, illustrated by this fictional encounter with a pastor and a faculty member at a Christian university. It is also to find and create models for a new relationship of cooperation in the twenty-first century. For this study, the geographical/ cultural context is primarily North American Christianity with a particular albeit not exclusive emphasis on evangelicalism. "Church" is herein defined largely in an institutional sense (the visible churches of the continent and their formal connections with each other) and is used to delineate both the "church at large" and specific denominational forms thereof. When possible, the word "denomination," although imperfect, is utilized to describe voluntary confessional groups. Finally, the "academy" is defined herein as "Christian higher education"; special attention is given to those institutions that are members of or similar in mission to the Council of Christian Colleges and Universities (CCCU).

Three institutions of higher education, along with their sponsoring denominations, have been identified for closer examination in this study. They are Eastern University, whose main campus is located in St. Davids, Pennsylvania; Huntington University, located in Huntington, Indiana; and George Fox University, located in Newberg, Oregon. They have been chosen for several reasons. The first is geographical diversity: one is on the East Coast, another in the Midwest, and the third on the West Coast. Access to the institutional leaders and familiarity with both mission and programs together constitute a second reason for choosing these three institutions: the author is a faculty member and former administrator for the first institution, an alumnus and former mid-level leader of the sponsoring denomination of the second, and an alumnus of the third.

All three are CCCU members but they reflect widely varying denominational sponsorships: Eastern is associated with the American Baptist Churches, USA; Huntington with the Church of the United Brethren in Christ, USA; and George Fox with the Evangelical Friends (Northwest Yearly Meeting). Finally, the three institutions have created very similar structures with three basic components: a core, residential undergraduate program in the arts and sciences; a more recent addition of graduate and professional studies programs; and a seminary or graduate school for the training of Christian ministers.

According to the CCCU, prior to the economic recession that began in 2008, Christian higher education in the United States had been "booming."[1] Composed in 2010 of 109 full-member and 69 affiliate-member institutions in North America and elsewhere, the organization boasted that enrollment statistics for their schools were far exceeding national trends in the United States. The CCCU was also touting positive trends in retention, loan repayment, aca-

1. Council for Christian Colleges and Universities, "The State of Christian Higher Education."

demic reputation, and caliber of students. The long-term results of the economic downturn are yet to be seen, and there is no doubt that Christian institutions, dependent as many are on tuition revenue, have suffered more deeply than many public institutions or those private universities with strong endowments. Nevertheless, despite any short-term downturn, there are consistent indicators that Christian higher education in the United States is healthy, prosperous, and growing.

The CCCU schools are currently identified in one way or another[2] with twenty-nine separate denominational or confessional groups.[3] However, the largest group, about a quarter of the total, is identified as having "no official denominational affiliation or religious affiliation." While some of the denominational affiliations are explicit from the names of the institutions (each of the eight Nazarene colleges includes the word "Nazarene" in its name), some of those that are included in CCCU statistics with a particular denominational branding do not otherwise publicly identify themselves as such. One way to ascertain the importance of such identity is to examine the institution's website, since the web represents the most common public gateway to institutional information in the twenty-first century and therefore constitutes the best evidence of an institution's self-identity. For instance, of the three institutions used as case studies for this project, each identifies itself explicitly as a Christian university but none identifies its denominational affiliation within its name or on the home page of its website.

Most Christian universities are growing and such growth is increasingly correlated with their ability to transcend fairly narrow denominational identities and market themselves to a wider Christian (and even non-Christian[4]) audience, as the opening nar-

2. The CCCU's data does not distinguish between denominational "ownership" on the one hand, and a mere "historical connection" on the other, so it is difficult to determine the depth of the relationship between the member schools and their sponsoring denominations without contacting the leaders of either party. Even then, one will sometimes get varying responses.

3. Council on Christian Colleges and Universities, 2009–2010 Profile.

4. For instance, my university does not require a faith commitment on

rative illustrates. This is particularly true for those institutions tied to smaller, less well-known, or more idiosyncratic denominations. And the relational stresses are not restricted to denominational schools; there are larger cultural and ideological forces at work that, for the past several decades, have created tensions between the Church in North America and the institutions of higher education founded by the church. Increasingly, academics and ministers find themselves sitting across a fence from each other, wondering what could possibly be motivating such unhelpful behavior on the other side.

WALKING THE WAY OF HOPE

Although certain external forces, including the decline in denominational identity, the power of market forces, and the growing philosophical/theological tensions between the lectern and the pulpit, have driven the academy and the church apart, the claim of this book is that these same forces can be harnessed to draw them closer together. The remainder of this study explores the forces that are affecting both the church and the academy and offers models for a more collaborative relationship in the twenty-first century.

Chapter 2, "Intersections on the Church's Journey," and Chapter 3, "Destinations on the Church's Journey," both explore the changing nature of the Church, specifically in the West but with references to the global Church as well. If it can be said that the focus of Chapter 2 is on "forces" or "tensions" (the word "intersection" is employed as a metaphor for the meeting of ideas), then Chapter 3 is concerned with "forms" or "practices" (the word "destination" is employed as a metaphor for how ideas are being translated into action). Neither chapter is exhaustive in its survey;

---

the part of its students and a significant minority of the adult students (who represent nearly 50% of the total student population) have either a nominal or non-existing faith commitment. The motives for this admission policy are both fiscal and evangelistic. They do see this as an opportunity to introduce these students to a faith-centered worldview and are fairly intentional about doing so.

such a study is beyond the scope of this project. Both, however, attempt to identify, primarily through the literature, some of the more relevant questions that are being asked and some of the transitions that are occurring.

Chapter 4, "Metaphors of the Academy's Journey," and Chapter 5, "Revolutions in the Academy's Journey," are intended as parallel discussions of the "forces and forms" of Christian higher education. Chapter 4 reviews the debate and the increasing literature on the relationship between church and academy in recent decades from the standpoint of the academy, using the concept of "metaphor" to explicate different understandings of that relationship. Chapter 5 reviews the rapidly changing forms of higher education in the United States and some of the implications that have arisen from the new delivery methods, market-driven methodologies, and student demographics that have characterized these forms.

Chapter 6, "Models of Church-Academy Collaboration" brings the twenty-first century church and the twenty-first century academy back together again in the same discussion to explore models by which these two institutional types may engage in a more collaborative relationship. For example, because denominational loyalties no longer limit relationships, a local church can partner with nearly any Christian university that can promise to provide an educational program specifically targeted to the needs of the church membership. And, because academic programs are no longer limited by geography, they can be marketed to distant populations, and even to small groups, for a limited time or for more permanent arrangements. Because academia often sees itself as a prophetic voice, the church can utilize academics in the role of consultants who will "speak the truth in love" to ministries that are in decline. And, because both churches and universities are increasingly committed to lifelong learning, they can work together to create programs for their (joint) adult populations that will address both spiritual and professional needs. This chapter uses current unique strengths from each of the three studied institutions to reveal how current structures can support collaboration and then provides two models of hypothetical universities created specifically within and for a twenty-first century context.

It is acknowledged that many churches and universities will decline to enter into such partnerships, either because of the mistrust already engendered over the past several decades or because of inflexible commitments to traditional forms of ministry or education. However, those that have already begun some level of reconfiguration and those that are willing to consider new forms for the twenty-first century will be able to tap into larger markets, more creative collaborations, more powerful offerings for their constituencies, and more opportunities for growth. In the end, those who will profit most will be students like Jimmy Long and Maria Hernandez.

2

Intersections on the Church's Journey

WALKING THE MIDDLE WAY

The "via media," the middle way, is usually regarded as the safe or true route between two dangerous options, the way to avoid the Scylla on the one side and the Charybdis on the other.[1] Aristotle's philosophy of the "golden mean," the policy that truth is usually found between two extremes, the appeal to moderation in all things, has greatly influenced this way of thinking. The prophets of the emerging church, on the other hand, are fond of noting that either/or reasoning is unnecessarily dichotomous, that very often truth is to be found in the tension of the both/and. One must

---

1. "In Greek mythology, Scylla and Charybdis were a pair of monsters who lived on opposite ends of the Strait of Messina between Italy and Sicily. Scylla was originally a sea nymph who was loved by the sea god Poseidon. Out of jealousy, Poseidon's wife Amphitrite poisoned the waters in which Scylla bathed. This turned Scylla into a six-headed beast with three rows of sharp teeth in each head. When ships passed close by her, she struck out to grab and eat unwary sailors. Charybdis was also a sea nymph, as well as the daughter of Poseidon. Zeus transformed her into a dangerous whirlpool across the strait from Scylla. Ships sailing the strait were almost certain to be destroyed by one of the monsters" ("Scylla and Charybdis," Encyclopedia of Myths, 2009, http://www.mythencyclopedia.com/Sa-Sp/Scylla-and-Charybdis.html).

wrap one's arms around both ends and embrace the middle.[2] And there is much in divine revelation that bears this out. God is one and God is three but He is certainly not merely two. The Kingdom of God has come, the Kingdom is near, and the Kingdom is yet to be realized. Christ is fully God; Christ is fully man. The mysteries of the faith lead us into dark alleys in which we unexpectedly discover marvelous entry halls into the Kingdom, entries that we would have missed had we stayed on the broad avenues of modernist rationalism.

And so it is here. The image used herein is that of the Christian pilgrim—an overused analogy, to be sure, but one with both historical and biblical precedents and one with the additional benefit of conveying a dynamic, as opposed to static, understanding of the faith.[3] The Kingdom of God is in motion. The Trinity is a verb.[4] And the via media is not the safe route between competing perils, but the route that permits the pilgrim to revel in the contradictions of the journey, to seek new sights and new adventures, and to establish new signposts on the way. From time to time, the pilgrim encounters an intersection, a place where roads to and from truth meet, an opportunity to travel in fresh directions. This chapter explores several such intersections that the Western Church, particularly the American Church, is likely to encounter in the twenty-first century. It concludes with a preliminary "roadmap" to assist others as they encounter these intersections on their own journeys.

2. "'The postmodern church, like the early church, lives in the 'both-and' of paradox. The emerging church celebrates mystery more than explanation. . . . For the leaders of tomorrow's church, this world of paradox represents an ancient-future church. It's stained glass *and* media screen. It's candles *and* stage lights together. It's secular *and* sacred." Slaughter and Bird, *Unlearning Church*, 45.

3. See Sweet, *Post-modern Pilgrims*.

4. This provocative statement is intended not as a principle of systematic theology, but as a critique of the notion of systematic theology, which must by definition assume a static context from which to construct the "systems" that such theological ruminations require. Systematic theology has its uses, but has perhaps achieved dominance in evangelical discussions of God that has hindered our ability to grasp his dynamism.

THE FIRST INTERSECTION: BEING AND DOING

This intersection is characterized by a negative observation: What the church *is* does not always correlate to what the church *does*. Its actions are not derived from its true identity; or, its true identity obscures its intended identity. Some believe but do not practice, resulting in behavior uncomfortably in sync with the world; others practice without holding fundamental beliefs, resulting in a purely civil or cultural religion. The intersection between the ontological and the methodological is inherently one of organic integrity. As Christ said, "Every good tree bears good fruit, but a bad tree bears bad fruit. A good tree cannot bear bad fruit and a bad tree cannot bear good fruit" (Matt 7:17–18). Even recognizing the eschatological dimensions of this tension, by which it is granted that the Church will not achieve the fullness of her calling until her final redemption,[5] few would argue that the Church in the West has experienced such integrity of identity and mission in recent years.[6]

The reasons for this are rooted both in human character and in Western assumptions of the church. More so than elsewhere, American Christianity has subscribed to a model of the church as "voluntary association." This model, which was one of the unintended consequences of the first Great Awakening,[7] encourages a

5. Albert Schweitzer, the famed early twentieth century missionary doctor, popularized an eschatological reading of the message, particularly the Kingdom ethics, of Jesus. See Schweitzer, *The Quest for the Historical Jesus*.

6. "There is a growing category of people who see themselves as spiritual but who are alienated from much traditional religion. Some of these people are actually in the Church, hanging on by their fingertips." Harries, *God Outside the Box*, xiii.

7. In another work, I traced the roots on this voluntaristic ecclesiology in the Presbyterian Church. The shift from the "parish model" occurred during the First Great Awakening, when revivalist preachers urged their listeners to forsake their unconverted ministers and join rival, revivalist churches that were often planted within the same parish. "The revivalists . . . had not only modified their understanding of conversion (soteriology) but had also taken a rather startling ecclesiological stance: they had transferred authority from the church, and by default, from the clergy, to the laity. . . . The revivalists had abruptly abandoned the ecclesiastical tradition of the Scots-Irish

competitive, even commercial, understanding of the church, as local congregations vie with each other—and with "worldly" enticements—for the temporary allegiance of families and individuals. It had a nineteenth century manifestation in the "new methods" of Charles Finney, who sought a scientific understanding of the morphology of conversion.[8] The competitive impulse resulted in certain new methodological strategies in the twentieth century as well, such as the church growth and church health movements.

One might argue that such a model is uniquely suited for the individualistic and mercantilist impulses of the American context and should therefore be examined and exploited. This argument is at the heart of the megachurch model.[9] However, such contextualization is achieved only at the risk of sacrificing the fundamentally organic and trinitarian nature of the Christian community and minimizing the essential work of the Spirit in the life of the church. The church's mystical strain, rooted in the pre-modern era, stands in sharp contrast to the method-driven assumptions of the modern era, which seeks a technology for everything, including the organic life of the Church.

A counter-cultural posture may be necessary in order for the Church to fulfill its prophetic, transformative role.[10] Such a posture has been advocated by Miroslav Volf, who has attempted to create a trinitarian understanding of the Church within a Protestant Free Church tradition.[11] Such trinitarian ecclesiologies have deep roots in the Eastern and even Roman traditions,[12] but have been

Presbyterians and had instead adopted the 'gathered church' model of the English Puritans" (Blair, "Scattered and Divided," 25).

8. See Hambrick-Stowe, *Charles G. Finney*; and Finney, *Lectures on Revival*. For a discussion of the Puritan understanding of the morphology of conversion (which Finney replaced), see Morgan, *Visible Saints*.

9. Schaller, *The Very Large Church*.

10. The language employed here is derived from H. Richard Niebuhr's classic *Christ and Culture*.

11. Volf, *After Our Likeness*. For a summary of his argument, see his chapter, "Community Formation as an Image of the Triune God" in Longenecker, *Community Formation in the Early Church and in the Church Today*, 213–38.

12. Volf utilizes the theological writings of Joseph Cardinal Ratzinger (now

notably absent in low-church Protestantism, which remains highly voluntaristic. Volf's thesis is that the community of the godhead, expressed as unity of purpose among plurality of persons, is a normative model for the community of faith that exists among the People of God. This model has significance for one's understanding of the role of the individual in community (see below) but also has implications for the mission of the Church in the world. If the church is a reflection, expression, or shadow of the Trinity, then its identity is somehow rooted in the incarnation. It becomes the likeness of God on earth; those who are in Christ are the physical manifestations of Christ in this era.

An incarnational church cannot be merely a voluntary collection of individuals; it is burdened with a revelatory responsibility to be Christ to those He loves. An incarnational church cannot be merely a refuge from the trials of the world; it is created with a calling to be in the world (believers are "cosmic invaders" in the enemy kingdom).[13] An incarnational church cannot be merely an organizational sponsor of "ministries" and "services;" it is gifted with a transformational power to change the world. In short, its praxis (methodology) is dependent upon its own understanding of its essence (ontology).[14]

Besides the trinitarian model, others are resurrecting the "bride" analogy to illustrate the relational aspect of the Church's relationship with God, and the implications of that "vertical" relationship for the "horizontal" relationships that take place within and among respective communities of faith. Radical Catholic

Pope Benedict XVI) to represent the Roman Catholic tradition and John D. Zizioulas (Metropolitan of Pergamon) to represent Orthodoxy.

13. One useful historical analogy here is to compare the work of several monastic orders. While the Benedictines sought withdrawal from the world, the Templars used coercion, the Franciscans modeled service, the Dominicans persuasion, and the Jesuits invasion. The Jesuits were the front line in the Catholic mission to evangelize the non-Western world. They followed or accompanied the conquistadors in every new arena.

14. See Sweet, *Jesus Drives Me Crazy*. A number of other works explore the concept of incarnational ministry. One of particular value to this author is Hiebert and Meneses, *Incarnational Ministry*.

activist Daniel Berrigan's *The Bride: Images of the Church* is one such example; Stephen Ayers' *Igniting Passion in Your Church* is another; a third is the postmodern "Prodigal Project" which, as its title suggests, derives inspiration from the story of the prodigal son returning to his loving, forgiving father.[15] The new evangelical emphasis on spiritual formation, led by Brennan Manning, Dallas Willard, Richard Foster, and others,[16] digs deeply in this vein, although too often their visions are limited to that of individual spirituality as opposed to the spiritual formation of the community of faith.

These works, and others like them, derive inspiration from the writings of medieval mystics, such as John of the Cross, Julian of Norwich, and Teresa of Avila.[17] John of the Cross, for instance, wrote famously of the "dark night of the soul" in language that bordered on eroticism. And, as Caroline Bynum has noted, some female mystics interpreted their status as the bride of Christ very literally, regarding the consumption of the transubstantiated elements—and sometimes even lactation—as an eroto-spiritual act.[18] One not plunge to this depth, however, to explore the workings of the Spirit in the love relationship that exists between the members of the godhead and, as the Church is drawn into God, between the Creator and the created. Leonard Sweet has termed believers who travel in this context "pneumanauts"—sailors of the Spirit. It is a marvelous juncture of the ontological and the methodological.

THE SECOND INTERSECTION: TRIBAL AND GLOBAL

There is but one Lord, one faith, and one baptism,[19] but there are plural Christianities. However, most articulations of this truism

15. Berrigan, *The Bride*; Ayers, *Igniting Passion in Your Church*; Riddell et al., *The Prodigal Project*.

16. See particularly Manning, *Ruthless Trust*; Willard, *The Divine Conspiracy*; and Foster, *Renovation of the Heart*.

17. See particularly John of the Cross, *The Dark Night of the Soul*; Furlong, *The Wisdom of Julian of Norwich*; and Teresa of Avila, *The Interior Castle*.

18. Bynum, *Holy Feast, Holy Fast*.

19. Ephesians 4:5.

delineate those Christianities into two corners of the global intersection—Jew and Gentile, orthodox and heretical,[20] catholic and apostate,[21] church and sect,[22] conservative and liberal, or, as Philip Jenkins has more recently proposed, the church of the West and the church of the "Global South."[23] This dichotomization of the faith which, as can be seen, is not the sole province of fundamentalists, has the advantage of simplicity but not of subtlety. It fails to recognize that there are multitudes of tribal expressions of faith, both in the West and elsewhere in the world. A bifurcative approach allows one the luxury of hegemony, by marginalizing minority institutions, or the facile assurance of truth, by regarding as illegitimate those expressions of the faith, of any size, that do not coincide with one's own.

A dichotomous understanding typically results in one of two responses—either an attempt to universalize one particular expres-

20. The study of heresy has become rather popular in recent years, as the word "heresy" itself is increasingly regarded by postmodern intellectuals as an anachronism at best and an expression of cultural hegemony at its worst. The latter interpretation is heavily dependent on Antonio Gramsci's work on hegemony. See Femia, *Gramsci's Political Thought*. There should still be room for heresy, however, even in a postmodern faith, if it were to be understood as occurring on a continuum on which all trust claims about God and His workings are to be located somewhere.

21. Since Vatican II, the Roman Catholic Church has created a third category for Protestant believers—"erring brethren."

22. These are two of the three types that were defined by Ernst Troeltsch: church, sect, and mysticism. Troeltsch, *The Social Teaching of the Christian Churches*. "Troeltsch distinguished between church, sect, and mysticism as primary types of religious life. The church is more peremptorily inclusive and achieves greater accommodation to worldly institutions. The sect demands voluntary commitment from its members, is more perfectionistic in its aims, and often adopts a critical stance toward existing social arrangements. Mysticism's individualistic and spiritualistic religiosity, to which Troeltsch himself was strongly attracted, is an ever present historical possibility, but it forges especially strong links with sect organizations and has a diffuse appeal under modern social conditions. These concepts have since become central to the sociological study of religious processes and have been variously adapted by more recent thinkers (e.g., H. Richard Niebuhr and Liston Pope)." Swatos, *Encyclopedia of Religion and Society*, no pages.

23. Jenkins, *The Next Christendom*.

sion of the faith (the Roman Catholic response) or an attempt to legitimize any and all expressions of Christianity, irrespective of their alignment with either biblical or historic roots (the hyper-ecumenist response). The first response is Platonic, in that it posits an "ideal" normative, accessible faith to which institutions and creedal statements must submit; the second response is Aristotelian, in that the faith is defined solely by the collection of its manifestations and not by an inherent unity. A third option is needed for a postmodern century. Such an option rejects Platonic idealism but need not succumb to mere nominalism; rather, it seeks the creative both/and of tolerance and conformity, of monism and pluralism, of diversity and unity.

The search for this third option may itself be an expression of idealism, yet the literature on faith in the emergent culture contains several such hopeful explorations. Dave Tomlinson's quest for a post-evangelical faith[24] and Brian McLaren's articulation of "a new kind of Christian" and "a generous orthodoxy"[25] are two examples of the attempt to transcend "conservative," "liberal," "evangelical," "fundamentalist" and other such defining (and confining) ideological labels. Others, such as George Yancey, Stephen Rhodes, Samuel Escobar, and Spencer Perkins and Chris Rice,[26] have presented models by which boundaries of race, culture, and ethnicity can be overcome within both global Christianity and local congregations.[27] Eastern Orthodoxy, which has historically attempted to empower national/tribal expressions of the Church without losing its universal character, has attracted the attention of a number of low-church Protestants within the past decade.[28] And

24. Tomlinson, *The Post-Evangelical*.

25. McLaren, *A New Kind of Christian; More Ready Than You Realize*; and *A Generous Orthodoxy*.

26. Yancey, *One Body, One Spirit*; Rhodes, *Where the Nations Meet*; Escobar, *The New Global Mission*; and Perkins and Rice, *More Than Equals*.

27. An excellent and well-studied model is the Mosaic church of Los Angeles, one of the largest and most innovative multiethnic churches in the United States. See Marti, *A Mosaic of Believers*.

28. Carroll, *The New Faithful*. A similar movement is occurring within Judaism. Klinghoffer, *The Lord Will Gather Me In*.

the multiple models for church structure (traditional, megachurch, house church, new monastic communities, etc.) available in the ecclesiastical marketplace provide a plethora of options for those interested in exploring alternative visions of the faith community.[29]

THE THIRD INTERSECTION:
EXCLUSION AND INCLUSION

It may be said that no group has an exclusive claim on attitudes of exclusivity. The role of religion in the "public square,"[30] the intersection where beliefs, values, ideas, and cultures meet, has been contentious from the beginning. The modernist notion of the separation of church and state—by which is usually meant the separation of "private" faith and "public" life—is remarkably new in the history of the world and remains somewhat counter-intuitive for the majority of the world's citizens, who have difficulty understanding how one can separate one's world view—with its perspectives, values, beliefs, ideas, and practices—from the means by which and the ends for which society is ordered and governed.[31]

The first years of the twenty-first century are therefore characterized by the intersection of two driving forces—a theocratic impulse, currently in abeyance in the West but triumphant in the Middle East and the Global South, and what John Finnis terms the "new secularism,"[32] an anti-religion posture that exceeds the theoretical neutrality of mere secularity. The "clash of civilizations" noted by Samuel Huntington[33] in the 1990s, prior to the wars

29. For an introduction to the house church movement, see Simson, *Houses That Change the World.*

30. The phrase is attributable to Richard John Neuhaus, *The Naked Public Square.*

31. Jenkins makes this argument in *The Next Christendom;* see particularly Chapter Seven, "God and the World," (141–62).

32. Finnis, "Secularism, Law, and Public Policy"; see also Finnis, *Moral Absolutes.*

33. Huntington, *The Clash of Civilizations.* See also Lewis, *What Went Wrong?*

against terrorism in the Middle East in this decade, is not between Islam on the one hand and Christianity on the other; rather, it is between radical theocracy and radical secularism, both of which are exclusivist positions. There is no middle ground. Islamic fundamentalists understand what many Westerners do not—that there no longer exists a "neutral" democratic, pluralist option by which Islam may peacefully co-exist with other viewpoints. If a "democratic Islam" is to be created, it must of necessity resemble either the secularity of the Western past or a fresh investiture of the naked public square.[34]

There is a growing consensus that the West is now experiencing something like a "second wave" of secularism. The first wave was largely supported by people of faith, for it assumed a neutral stance toward religion and permitted its free expression. The anti-religious tenor of the second wave is rooted, according to Roger Scruton, in a desire for transcendence.[35] The gap created by the effective banishment of religion from public life is being replaced by a new religion of secularism. Scruton and James Kurth have both noted, *a la* Rene Girard,[36] that, like Christianity, this new de-sacralized secularism required widespread human sacrifice in the latter half of the twentieth century—in the form of abortion victims, anti-religious bigotry, and widespread martyrdom by communist government.[37] Alvin Platinga distinguishes between the two forms of secularism in terms of their relationship to science: the "older" secularism was supportive of scientific inquiry, with which it assumed a theoretically objective stance, while the newer secularism is inherently hostile to science, as it is to religion, presumably because of its pretenses to transcendence.[38] Neuhaus argues that religious people can accommodate a secular worldview,

34. See Roy, *Globalised Islam*.

35. Scruton, "Clash of Worldviews"; see also Scruton, *The Meaning of Conservatism*.

36. Girard, *Things Hidden Since the Beginning of the World*.

37. Kurth, "Clash of Worldviews."

38. Plantinga, "Science and Secularism"; see also Sennett, *The Analytic Theist*.

but secularists of the newer variety cannot accommodate religious viewpoints.[39]

A new secularism requires a creative Christian response, one or more "third" options that reject both theocracy and irrelevance. Those options must be defined by a new pluralism that accommodates multiple ideologies without taking sides and without expelling others from "the marketplace of ideas." This implies a necessary rejection of the secularist claims of neutrality. As John Finnis notes, rejection of the idea of the soul as the organizing principle of the human results in the inability to affirm the equality of persons, among other supposed principles of secularism, thus making secularism inadequate as a basic for law or civil society.[40] But the articulation of a third option also implies a necessary rejection of theocracy, and especially any supposed correlation between theocracy and democracy. As countless historical examples illustrate, a theocratic society cannot help but be an intolerant society, and that intolerance extends not only to unbelievers but also to believers of other stripes.

A creative route through the intersection of exclusion and inclusion may not, in the end, be discovered in the West, where the battle lines are longstanding and the memories fierce. There is hope, however, for such creativity to merge somewhere in the Global South or East, in a context that values both the role of religion in public life and the benefits of ideological diversity. If it is to occur in the West, it will be at an intersection where both church and academy and present and engaged.

THE FOURTH INTERSECTION:
INDIVIDUAL AND COMMUNITY

On one corner of this intersection, there exists a secular, and increasingly Christian, idea of the autonomy of the individual, which results in a purely voluntaristic faith, as noted earlier. This concept of autonomy has deep roots in Western culture; its origins

39. Neuhaus, "Secularism, Law, and Public Policy."

40. Finnis, 2003.

are the subject of much debate. It has origins in and continues to draw strength from classical Greek rationalism,[41] the theology of Augustine,[42] the appeal to individual conscience by the Protestant reformers,[43] Renaissance notions of art and action as the work of individuals,[44] Adam Smith's economic morality,[45] the poetry and stories of the Romantics, and, more recently, the ethos of existentialism.[46] The culture of postmodernism runs the risk of reinforcing this tendency toward autonomy by locating truth within the self.

On another corner one can discern a number of counterbalancing communitarian influences, even in the West. In fact, one might argue that the communitarian impulse was the stronger at least through the first half of the twenty-first century. It manifested itself in Spartan notions of duty, Roman conceptions of citizenship, late Roman and early medieval Germanic understandings of the tribe, the claims to universality and uniformity in the Church of the high medieval era, the nationalism of the early modern period, occasional experiments in communal utopias,[47] Marxist

41. There is, of course, a tension between the autonomous moral conscience of Socrates and the implied collectiveness of Plato in classical Greek philosophy. Plato, *Apology* . . . .

42. Augustine is usually regarded as the first autobiographer in the West. Augustine, *Confessions*.

43. This is particularly true in the thinking and writing of Martin Luther.

44. The fourteenth-century Italian writer Petrarch is sometimes regarded as the first true individualist.

45. See Smith, *The Wealth of Nations*.

46. Jean-Paul Sartre, in particular, was torn between the principle of individual authenticity and the lure of the collective, particularly in its Marxist dress. Martin Buber is another existentialist who explored the relations of the autonomous self. See Sartre, *Existentialism and Humanism*; Buber, *I and Thou*.

47. Examples include Thomas More's "Utopia", the Ephrata (Pennsylvania) Cloister, New Harmony (in Pennsylvania and Indiana), the Oneida Colony (New York), and even the founding visions of Philadelphia and Boston. For a comparative study of the competing utopian visions of these two cities, see Baltzell, *Puritan Boston and Quaker Philadelphia*.

socialism,[48] and, most noticeably, Fascism.[49] There is little doubt, however, that in the United States at least, the individualistic impulse is in the ascendance.[50]

This longstanding cultural tension preceded and has significantly influenced the Church. One could argue that the distinction between "high church" and "low church" structures is not primarily liturgical, but relational, in the sense that high church structures are hierarchical and extra-congregational, whereas low church structures are democratic and local. This is, however, an over-generalization, as there are a varieties of structures, especially within the Reformed tradition, that attempt to mediate between the two, principally by dividing authority between the local congregation and some regional body. Volf, as noted earlier, seeks to maintain a "free church" ecclesiology (in the spirit of John Smyth) within a trinitarian framework. In so doing, he locates the individual believer within the collective, thus obliterating notions of individual autonomy without negating the unique calling of the individual within the Kingdom of God. This approach does not resolve all arguments. Volf is least convincing when he explicates the relationship of the local congregation to the Church Universal. But it is one notable attempt at a via media in the intersection between individualism and communitarianism in the Church.

Another creative route through this intersection is that employed by the philosopher Alasdair MacIntyre. MacIntyre's career has been largely given to a multifaceted critique of the "modernist project." In his more recent works, however, the influence of

48. Marxism could be regarded as the triumph of the collectivist or communitarian spirit.

49. Mussolini's notion of the individual finding its identity and expression only in the state is the best articulation of this. The argument is, ironically, quite similar to high-church ecclesiologies, in which the individual believer finds his or her identity and role only in the Church.

50. One might argue that one reason for the apparent rift in current relations between the U.S. and some of the nations of Europe is due to a lingering (or growing) communitarism in Europe, manifest in the growth of the European Union and in an implicit acknowledgement of the sovereignty of the United Nations over the modern nation-state.

Thomism on his thinking has been more pronounced.[51] Perhaps MacIntyre's chief contribution has been to reject Enlightenment notions of rational objectivism without succumbing to radical, individualistic subjectivism. Instead, he roots rationality, justice, and other such transcendent ideals within traditions; in effect, he encourages communities to create, define, maintain, and even propagate their understandings of these ideals rather than abandon them entirely as a result of the demise of Enlightenment notions of objectivity. He even advocates a process by which communities can dialogue and even persuade others of the pragmatism, if not the correctness, of their respective understandings, even without an appeal to an objective standard.[52]

Volf's ecclesiological route and MacIntyre's philosophical path represent but two options for a via media at the intersection of individualism and communitarianism. Other options can and will be created.

THE FIFTH INTERSECTION: WORD AND FEELING

On one corner of this intersection there is situated a modern culture, impacted by both the testimony of written revelation and a commitment to rational, propositional truth; in short, it is a logocentric culture. On another corner, there exist both premodern and postmodern rejections of this culture; instead, there has been built a culture that focuses on the senses, imagination, sound, and mystery as expressions of truth and faith. The latter corner represents a new Romanticism, different from its nineteenth century predecessor only in that it is devoid of the former's idealism. Sweet characterizes this emerging culture with the acronym "epic"—it is experiential, participatory, image-driven, and connected.[53] This culture would prefer to participate rather than listen, experience

---

51. Murphy, *Alasdair MacIntyre*.

52. MacIntyre, *Whose Justice? Which Rationality?*

53. Sweet, *Soul Tsunami*; and *A Cup of Coffee at the Soul Café*.

rather than reason, view images rather than words, and create connections rather than structures.[54]

While there are many dynamics at work here, this intersection particularly reveals one of the weaknesses of Western
philosophy—its historically narrow understanding of epistemology. One could argue that Western history has been dominated
by four particular strands of epistemology: authority, rationality,
empiricism, and intuition. In fact, the history of Western thought
may be characterized by the interplay of these (often competing)
epistemological traditions. For instance, the medieval era was
characterized by appeals to and structures of authority, to which
was contrasted the empiricism of the Scientific Revolution, resulting in famous clashes like that of Galileo and Pope Urban VIII.
The Romantic era, with its reliance on intuition (feeling, emotion,
and mystery) was a reaction to an over-indulgence in rationalism
during the era of the Enlightenment. The history of the twentieth
century was, to some degree, a history of conflicts between these
competing epistemologies.

At the beginning of the twenty-first century one finds a
similar interplay between the cultural and ideological forces of
premodernism, modernism, and postmodernism in the church.
Premodernism, which is still a powerful force within evangelicalism, Roman Catholicism, and Orthodoxy, rooted as they are in tradition and a biblical worldview, relies heavily on appeals to biblical
or ecclesiastical authority. Modernism, dominant among the mainstream Protestant churches, is rational to its core. And postmodernism, which is making inroads into all of these traditions, gives great

54. For a Jewish example of the growing literature on experiencing God, see
Goldstein, *God at the Edge*. Attempts to delineate or define "postmodern culture" have been problematic. A purely sociological identification would note
that postmodern attitudes may be particularly observed among Generation
X, urbanites, and those who have experienced a cosmopolitan lifestyle. A cultural definition would note that the ideas and attitudes of postmodernism
are dominant in the mainstream media and are therefore emblematic of early
twenty-first century mainstream culture. A philosophical definition would
note that the major thinkers of the late twentieth century were in some way
postmodernist but that these ideas are still largely confined to the academy.

credence to experiential knowledge. All three of these forces are simultaneously present in the Church, and great energy is expended in defending one against the others or promoting one at the expense of the others, when each cultural understanding may be appropriate for its own audience and an appreciation of all three may be most valuable in ascertaining the breadth of God's Kingdom. In short, an epistemological imperative[55] for the twenty-first century is to utilize all valid epistemological options simultaneously in order to comprehend the fullness of the truth that is ultimately God's.[56]

An illuminating discussion on these lines was conducted by Andy Crouch, Michael Horton, Frederica Mathewes-Green, Brian D. McLaren, and Erwin Raphael McManus in *The Church in Emerging Culture*.[57] Each of these articulate individuals represents a variation in the spectrum of contemporary Christian approaches to the interplay of faith and culture, of truth and meaning. They do not agree with each other, but their respect for each other's understandings and their willingness to humble themselves before the other, to learn and be corrected by the insights of others, gives hope that a new route can be charted through the intersection of logocentrism and the new romanticism in the twenty-first century.

THE MIDDLE WAY: A PRELIMINARY ROADMAP

At the conclusion at this brief survey of the anticipated intersections of the Church's twenty-first century, one may begin to construct a roadmap for a via media. That middle way will likely be characterized by the following.

Multiplicity

I am not recommending a particular via media; there are multiple roads and multiple intersections. The preceding pages highlighted

55. I shamelessly borrow from Kant's "categorical imperative" in creating this term. See Kant, *Groundwork of the Metaphysics of Morals*.

56. See Holmes, *All Truth is God's Truth*.

57. Sweet, *The Church in Emerging Culture*.

several that are of particular interest to this author and the larger project to which this particular discussion is one component. Others will begin at different starting-points and arrive at different intersections, or will perhaps approach these same intersections from a different direction and thus offer an additional perspective to this study.[58]

Incarnation

The via media can be plotted in advance and can be imagined, but it can only become real to those who physically travel it. The hope of believers is that their Savior has traveled the road ahead of them, that He has made their path straight and that the signposts He has placed along the way are trustworthy. He has not asked them to remove themselves from the journey; rather, as they are in Him and He is in them,[59] they represent Him to others on the road. To use biblical language, believers are called into the world, not out of it.

Dynamism

The Kingdom of God is in motion because God is in motion. Much of the systematic theology of the past is rooted in a static notion of the godhead, which spilled over into a static notion of the people of God. The resultant organizational paradigms for the Church have hindered the People of God from perceiving their identity in organic, growing, moving terms. They will discover their identity as pilgrims when they realize they are on a journey.

Community

This word, like others in this volume, is over-used. New language is needed to articulate fresh conceptions of tired ideas for a twenty-

58. The multiplicity of visions for the church of the future is evident in the literature on the twenty-first century church. One may wish to compare the following: Towns and Bird, *Into the Future*; Gibbs, *ChurchNext*; Stanley, *The Next Generation Leader*; and Anderson, *A Church for the Twenty-First Century*.

59. The "high-priestly" prayer of Jesus in John 17.

first century audience. Nevertheless, it is necessary to note there that the via media is one that is not walked alone. Communities of faith, communities of inquiry, communities of tradition, communities of nations, communities of practice[60]—all of these together present the corporate entities in which the individual believer creates and finds one's own identity, mission, and roadmap. God always has a People.

Creation

The roads are not yet all built; the intersections are not yet all defined. The God who is the Creator of the universe imbues His People with aspects of that creative impulse in order to seek new paths in the wilderness. To change the analogy, in the face of those who argue that the truth has been once delivered, that the house has been constructed and must merely be maintained, God's creative people search in dusty attics and well-stocked closets and under the furniture for treasures forgotten or never yet seen.

Other attributes are yet to be defined, and when all are defined, the Kingdom of God in motion will create new intersections and new via media for the pilgrim to travel. The journey is ongoing until the end of all things and the beginning of all hopes are realized.

60. For this concept, see Wenger, *Communities of Practice.*

3

Destinations on the Church's Journey

WALKING THE LONG WAY

THE LONG way is the trail on which the People of God have been journeying since the Fall. The road to our final redemption is one for the persistent, for its length has been measured in epochs rather than generations or miles. Those of the old covenant waited in patient longing for their redeemer to visit them, and though they waited with faith, few lived to see the desires of their hearts.[1] Those of the new covenant look back now two millennia to the generation during which the already-but-not-yet kingdom of God invaded the world, and wonder aloud at how much further the road ahead will take them. "How long, how long must we sing this song?"[2] Our song is new to the ears of a listening world but is very, very ancient to those who sing it daily to our God.[3]

And yet the ending of the song is very near. Or, to revert to the original metaphor, the road may yet end around the very next bend. One is never sure whether this is the final stage of the journey. And so we walk with gladness on our countenance and hope in

---

1. This is the message of Hebrews 11—those of the old covenant who lived by faith even though they were denied the privilege of seeing its fulfillment.

2. Lyrics from "Sunday, Bloody Sunday," by the Irish rock group U2.

3. Psalm 40:3—"I will sing a new song unto the Lord."

our hearts, for today may be the day in which all things promised will come to pass. Those of the original kingdom generation believed it to be imminent in their time;[4] those of many intervening generations considered themselves the last to inhabit this dying planet. Those of our generation—and perhaps many generations to come—live in anticipation of the final consummation, while yet taking joy in the journey.[5] All who are pilgrims in this journey are invited to take joy in the experience of its passage, not merely in the eventual arrival at their destinations.

The thesis of this chapter is that there are multiple destinations for this generation of the Church. Some are merely mile markers on the road to further frontiers; others are places to which we are called to arrive and stay. Some involve some measure of revisiting sites already marked by those who came before, for the purpose of retracing paths of promise or for the need to reverse direction on trails that have led us nowhere.[6] Some destinations are unique to the American church; others are universal for all who are pilgrims in the kingdom. In any case, our destinations are not our own choosing; they are places to which we are called, should we choose to go. Let's explore three such destinations that are of particular value to the twenty-first century church.

THE FIRST DESTINATION:
A NEW DEFINITION OF CHURCH

We all know what a church is. A church is a building with a steeple, located usually in some quiet suburban neighborhood or on a country road. A church is an organization led by a pastor or a

---

4. As noted earlier, this was the eschatological thesis of the theologian Albert Schweitzer—that the original generation, Jesus included, expected the final consummation within their own generation.

5. "There is a joy in the journey. There's a light we can love on the way." Lyrics from "Joy in the Journey" by Michael Card.

6. This statement reflects the "ancient/future" dimension of the emergent church, as defined by Leonard Sweet, Robert Webber, and others. See Webber, *Ancient-Future Faith.*

priest or a vicar, and it dispenses "religious" services and products of the peculiarly Christian brand. A church is a place to which one goes to acquire such products and services, be they peace of mind or an experience of the transcendent or a connection with fellow believers. A church is a legally recognized nonprofit entity with special exemptions from taxation and with a privileged role in American society.

These definitions reflect cultural and legal understandings of the church, as it has been understood in American society. There is a growing recognition that "church" does not always look like this, but the exceptions to the rule often serve merely to reinforce the normative nature of the rule. Those who would do things differently must provide justification for their differing or suffer the reproach of the majority. Fortunately, there are increasing numbers of those who have taken the risk of subverting the dominant paradigm in search of alternate, multiple, or even more biblical models of local church ministry.

One of the greatest challenges in re-defining the church is the issue of size, in large part because the church growth movement of the past generation emphasized numerical growth as the predominant indicator of biblical fidelity.[7] The church health movement, of more recent vintage, has sought a broader understanding of church life by articulating multiple manifestations of healthy, organic church growth.[8] One of the most popular prophets of this movement is the German sociologist Christian Schwarz, whose study of growing churches in six continents resulted in his identification of eight traits of a healthy church ministry—and a self-evaluation tool by which congregations can measure their own healthiness in

7. The church growth movement was largely pioneered by Donald A. McGavran and C. Peter Wagner from Fuller Theological Seminary in the late 1970s. MacGavran and Wagner, *Understanding Church Growth*. Both MacGavran and Wagner later protested the degree to which their arguments were used by others in support of a single focus on numerical growth.

8. This movement probably originated in popular form in the "Growing a Healthy Church" series by the SonLife organization. See Spader and Mayes, *Growing a Healthy Church*.

comparison with others.[9] There is something of a tautological flaw in Schwarz's approach—the eight traits were drawn from observing churches he had subjectively regarded as healthy, and then applied as normative to others—yet there has been great value his organic, as opposed to organizational, approach to church growth.[10]

Both movements have tended to reinforce, intentionally or inadvertently, the notion of the large, growing church as the normative biblical model. Whereas the heroes of American religious culture from the 1950s through the early 1980s were itinerant evangelists, radio preachers or televangelists,[11] the heroes of American evangelicalism in the past few decades have been largely the pastors of the new "mega-churches" that dot the American landscape. Bill Hybels of Willow Creek Community, Rick Warren of Saddleback, D. James Kennedy (now deceased) of Coral Ridge Presbyterian, T. D. Jakes of the Potter's House, Joel Osteen of Lakewood Church, Robert Schuller of The Crystal Cathedral, and others of their ilk become household names across the country and, in some cases, across the world.[12] There are many others waiting in the wings for the opportunity to wear the mantle of leadership in the mega-church movement.

Against this backdrop of "largeness," there are those with the courage to preach a gospel of smallness, at least in terms of church size. Lyle Schaller's *The Small Church is Different*,[13] was an early recognition that the average community church in the

9. See Schwarz, *Natural Church Development*.

10. One of the first to articulate this organic understanding of church life was Larry Richards, whose works were required reading in many college Bible departments in the 1980s. See Richards, *A Theology of Christian Education;* and Richards and Hoeldtke, *A Theology of Church Leadership*.

11. One thinks here of Fulton Sheen, Norman Vincent Peale, Billy Graham, Jimmy Swaggart, Pat Robertson, Jerry Falwell, and others. This is not to imply that those still active have lost their popularity, but it can be argued that they are regarded less as driving forces in evangelical culture and more as respected artifacts of a time that we remember fondly.

12. Interestingly, a few of these have combined megachurch ministries with media savvy, particularly Kennedy, Jakes, and now Joel Osteen.

13. Schaller, *The Small Church is Different*.

United States was relatively small and that this was not necessarily an indication of weakness. In the last two decades, there have been few prominent voices raised in support of the smaller church, in part because small was counter-cultural in American consumerist society and in part because the critics of the small church were largely right: Most of the small congregations in the United States were so not because of choice but because of the loss of parishioners, particularly younger members, due to a failure to remain missional in a changing culture.[14]

The house church movement seeks to change that perception. Its prophets (Wolfgang Simson, Robert Fitts, Larry Kreider, et al.) are not yet household names, and the movement is still attempting to extract itself from the contrarian, anti-denominational, rabidly independent character it had previously acquired. Simson, for one, has provided a solid theological framework for the movement, supported by an historical analysis that seeks the roots of the decline of authentic New Testament Christianity in the Constantinian accommodations that resulted in the erection of public houses of worship.[15] Kreider seeks to change the perception of the house church movement—and mitigate against its frequent excesses—by partnering house churches with traditional community churches or, at the very least, with each other.[16] Bob Fitts has attempted to link house churches together by appointing coordinators for each of the U.S. states and even by county, when possible.[17]

Another movement that represents a creative middle ground between the house church and the megachurch is the cell church movement. Based on this researcher's personal observations, the cell church model has become the dominant preference of church planters in the United States (and elsewhere) within the past decade.

14. See here Anderson, *Dying for Change* and *A Church for the 21st Century* as examples of this literature.

15. Simson, *Houses That Change the World*.

16. Kreider and Wagner, *House Church Networks*; Kreider et al., *New House Church Networks*. Kreider is the founder of Dove Christian Fellowship International, Lititz, Pennsylvania.

17. Fitts, *The Church in the House*.

In the cell church, the small group (the cell) becomes the primary ministry unit and the primary context for relationships. The cells are brought together for "congregation" or "celebration."[18] A number of traditional churches have sought to realign themselves as cell churches, which has proven to be a difficult task.[19] Nevertheless, there are those who believe that such realignments are critical for the American church to be culturally relevant in the coming generation.[20]

Any particular structural model is bound to disappoint if it is adopted merely for utilitarian purposes; e.g. for purposes of numerical growth or cultural adaptation. The principles underlying the new models are more foundational than the models themselves, and can be articulated in two words: relationship and incarnation. Relational models are, by definition, structured in such a way as to encourage intimacy between individuals, as individuals on the same journey, and intimacy with God, as one who is real in this world.[21] Incarnational models are those that seek to invade the culture, to be physically present where people live and work, rather than require those people to withdraw themselves from the world in order to meet and know God. Michael Frost and Alan Hirsch capture this tension well when they distinguish between incarnational and attractional models of ministry.[22] The attractional model, which is inherent in the megachurch movement, calls people out of the world to a large physical plant in which is offered a plethora of religious services. The incarnational model, inherent in the house church movement and elsewhere, sends people into the world to be Christ among the redeemable.

18. See Neighbour, *Where Do We Go From Here?*

19. I am personally aware of several churches that have rather intentionally and rather ruthlessly transitioned from a traditional format to a cell-based structure. All have lost members, at least in the short term.

20. See, for instance, Stockstill, *The Cell Church.*

21. See Sweet, *Out of the Question . . . Into the Mystery.*

22. Frost and Hirsch, *The Shaping of Things to Come,* 18–20. Frost and Hirsch describe the contemporary church as "attractional, dualistic, and hierarchical."

This is not to argue that the attractional model is illegitimate or without merit. In fact, it has proven to be surprisingly attractive to large numbers of Western Christians, particularly Americans and particularly baby boomers, in the late twentieth century and has admittedly been an instrument for the conversion of many who would probably not been won through traditional community churches. Its success, however, has given it a dominance in the cultural landscape that has obscured other models, particularly the incarnational model discussed here. The two models working in concert would have a more powerful impact than either of them do alone.

THE SECOND DESTINATION: A NEW UNDERSTANDING OF DENOMINATIONALISM

Among the difficulties in pursuing these new models are institutional barriers erected by traditional denominationalism. The denomination in which this author holds his ordination, for instance, officially recognizes a church only after it has attained an average annual worship attendance of fifty persons and has ten resident member families.[23] This definition excludes house churches from legitimacy simply by virtue of size. Congregations that are forsaking the concept of "membership" in preference for other relational covenants are likewise excluded. One might argue (and some have) that the biblical definition of a church is two or three believers gathered in the name of Christ.[24] The reasons for enlarging that definition are partially legal (because of the protected status of churches in the United States) and in part cultural. We assume a certain minimal size in our cultural understanding of church. That theoretical minimum is largely derived from our notions of professional ministry, which are discussed in a later section of this chapter.

There is significant and well-known statistical evidence that the mainline or historic denominations of the West are, as a whole,

---

23. *Discipline of the Church of the United Brethren in Christ USA.*

24. See, for instance, Volf, *After Our Likeness.*

struggling to maintain membership.[25] And there is sufficient sociological analysis to help us ascertain reasons for this decline.[26] It can be argued that denominationalism is a uniquely American creation, born out of the pluralism of American colonial life and the competitiveness of the first Great Awakening.[27] If so, there is nothing particularly sacred about it that demands its maintenance or survival in the face of competing paradigms.

And yet it seems that even those most bitterly opposed to denominationalism find themselves creating structures that resemble denominations in many respects. Seventeenth century Congregationalists created unions of churches that functioned much like presbyteries. The original United Brethren became The Moravian Church. Those who chose the same name in the mid-eighteenth century were a hodgepodge collection of German revivalists dismissed from or made uncomfortable in their home denominations who nevertheless organized themselves into an institution by 1815. Baptists or nearly all stripes created conventions and associations that are perceived as denominational by observers even if not denoted as such by their participants. The Bible Church, Vineyard, and Calvary Chapel movements began as networks of likeminded congregations but are today probably best described as denominations. As noted previously, even the house church movement is finding it necessary to abandon its anti-denominational outlook and to create, at the very least, linkages and perhaps even a nascent national organization.[28]

If denominationalism can be described as a response to the need to affiliate, officially or otherwise, with churches that share

25. Statistical evidence for this trend is plentiful. One of the most illuminating ways to observe the patterns is to compare sequential editions of Mead's *Handbook of Denominations*, now in its 11th edition. There are, of course, exceptions to the rule.

26. See, for instance, Barna, *The Second Coming of the Church*; and, more recently, Wolfe, *The Transformation of American Religion*.

27. As noted, I have made such an argument regarding the Presbyterian movement in America (Blair, "Scattered and Divided").

28. The house church network has an online hub at www.house2house.net.

similar beliefs, practices, or values, then those who have announced the arrival of the era of post-denominationalism will find themselves disappointed. If, on the other hand, denominationalism must be described as a hierarchical model of geographically-related congregations, then it will face some serious challenges in the twenty-first century. As Frost and Hirsch have observed, the hierarchical nature of the church, including its connectional structures, represents one of its cultural accommodations and thus one of its limitations for ministry in the emergent culture.[29]

The relationship between geography and church structure represents one of the largely ignored phenomena of the emerging paradigm. The European model of the local congregation was that of the parish, a collection of people defined by geographical boundaries; one's congregational membership was determined by the location of one's residence. This model was transplanted to the American colonies by Puritans, Presbyterians, Anglicans, and Lutherans. However, the revivals of the mid-eighteenth century divided most of these fledgling denominations into partisan networks (e.g., "Old Sides" vs. "New Sides," "Old Lights" vs. "New Lights") that ignored parish boundaries to plant competing congregations in the same geographical area. By so doing, power was transferred from clergy to laity, for it was the laity who decided in those situations to which church they would belong and which minister they would hear.[30] American religious pluralism was transformed into American religious capitalism, in which competition determined which churches would survive or thrive in the marketplace of spirituality. This pattern has remained largely unchanged.

Denominational structures, however, for the most part have not yet undergone a similar transformation. Most are still organized by geography—into districts, conferences, synods, annual meetings, or other such judicatory divisions. Perhaps it is time for denominations to reorganize themselves. There are several options

---

29. Frost and Hirsch, *The Shaping of Things to Come*, 18–20.

30. For a book-length treatment of this thesis, see Westerkamp, *Triumph of the Laity*.

available to them. One such option is the affinity group, which is a voluntary association of congregations and/or ministers who share something significant in common—ministry philosophy, size, demographic setting, mission, etc.—but who are not necessarily located near each other.[31] This model was not feasible until the current generation because limitations of communication and transportation technology made accountable relationships at a distance difficult.[32] A denomination of affinity groups would not be entirely unusual. Most denominations are organized geographically; a denomination organized by affinity would transcend geography to group likeminded or similar churches together into districts, conferences, presbyteries, or whatever form of mid-level judicatory is used by each particular tradition.

Another option is the multi-denominational geographical approach, in which likeminded congregations and/or ministers within a defined geographical area join forces to accomplish a common mission. This was the original motivation of the community ministerium, which remains a feature of many small and mid-sized towns but which has been frequently criticized for an excessive ecumenism that unites around the lowest common denominator, rather than a transformational mission. Other parallel structures, consisting primarily of evangelicals, have been created in many U.S. cities, some with great missional intentionality, such as Mission Columbia in South Carolina. This interdenominational group dedicated itself to the 800,000 souls in metropolitan Columbia and agreed to partner instead of compete with each other in achieving that mission, under the realization that no one church can do this alone.[33]

---

31. Adams, *Voluntary Associations*.

32. Maintaining organizations across great distances is the topic of much management literature. One popular volume is Kostner, *Virtual Leadership*. One model of an affinity group is the Willow Creek Association, which has attracted congregations from multiple denominational and non-denominational affiliations to join together in implementation of a common ministry philosophy. See www.willowcreek.com.

33. Jeff Shipman, pastor of Columbia Crossroads Church, interviewed 2

Such interdenominational relationships and non-geographical alignments will require denominations to examine their definitions of and motivations for exclusivity. Exclusivity reflects a gate-keeping approach to institutional identity—one's institution is defined by who or what is excluded from membership or participation.[34] While it is true that exclusivity cannot be entirely eliminated—otherwise there would remain no means of establishing unique identities—it is also true that organizations possess both positive and negative identity traits. An historical pattern of primarily negative identification has proven to be one of the most significant barriers to the realization of Jesus' prayer for the unity of His church (John 17).

THE THIRD DESTINATION: A NEW DEFINITION
OF PROFESSIONAL MINISTRY

The very concept of "professional" ministry has come under attack in recent years. John Piper rails against the term in his polemical *Brothers, We Are Not Professionals*.[35] The numerical growth of independent churches, the parachurch phenomenon, the growth of ministry specializations, and a rising anti-denominational fervor have all contributed to redefining both the role of the professional minister and the credentials required in order to occupy or fulfill that role in American culture. As a result, it has become increasingly difficult to define exactly what a professional minister is and who is worthy of such appellation. This is a good thing. For the purposes of this chapter, professional ministers will be defined as those who either receive payment for the religious services

---

April 2004 in Middletown, Pennsylvania. Shipman is an ordained Missionary Church minister who was then part of a four-man leadership team of an Evangelical Free Church in Columbia that has already planted several daughter churches with different denominational affiliations.

34. Antonio Gramsci provided a sociological basis for this phenomenon—the desire for hegemony that causes one to marginalize those who are defined as external to the dominant group. See Forgacs, *The Antonio Gramsci Reader*.

35. Piper, *Brothers, We Are Not Professionals*.

rendered or who have been granted some kind of official status as clergy among their constituent groups.[36]

It is difficult to make an argument from history against the concept of professional clergy. Since civilization was first introduced as a result of the agricultural revolution, every society has had those who shared specialized religious knowledge or practices in exchange for a portion of the surplus economy of that society. The Israelites were not merely permitted, but actually commanded, to establish a professional priesthood to be supported by the mandatory contributions of the people. The model Jesus adopted for his ministry was that of the professional peripatetic rabbi of first century Judea. The early apostles could be defined as professionals as well, for even when they earned their living plying their original vocations, they advocated their right to earn money from their ministry (see 1 Cor 9). In subsequent centuries, the Christian priesthood was modeled largely after the priesthood of the Roman *cultus*, and its clergy were increasingly professionalized.

Nevertheless, it has been occasionally difficult to meld these practices with the biblical concept of the priesthood of all believers, which became one of the fresh discoveries and rallying cries of the Protestant Reformation. Luther and the other major reformers restored the principle of individual access to God the Father through the mediation of Christ alone, but maintained the professional clergy as either instruments for the transmission of grace, pastors of the Lord's flock, or teachers of the faithful. In the American context, the role of the professional minister has undergone a significant four-step transformation over the past quarter millennium based largely on broader cultural currents.

The colonial understanding of the pastor as "spiritual director" or "village theologian," in which his primary responsibility was to preach and catechize the congregation, was replaced in the nineteenth century with the model of pastor as "spiritual physician," in

---

36. "A cleric who feeds the sheep of a single congregation in order that the sheep might also feed, clothe, and house him" is the definition offered by Keizer, "Career Ministry," 30–33.

which the pastor was expected to visit the sick and otherwise care for even the physical needs of one's flock. After World War II, the pastor also became a "spiritual counselor" as the psychological disciplines gained prominence in American culture. And, finally, about a generation ago the model of "the pastor as spiritual CEO," which emphasizes organizational leadership dynamics, became dominant and has remained so.[37] Interestingly, each of the later roles did not replace but merely supplemented the previous roles, to the point where the typical American pastor of the early twenty-first century is burdened with cultural expectations that exceed the giftedness or competencies of any particular individual. The attrition rate is high.

The responses to this dilemma have been several. First, the megachurch model has resulted in the specialization of professional ministry, by function or even age group. This has released ministers to serve within their area of gifting or calling, without requiring them to become "general practitioners," which had hitherto been the dominant cultural paradigm.[38]

Second, the new church planting and house church movements have created a fresh wave of bivocational ministers, sometimes called "tentmakers" in deference to the Apostle Paul's practice of plying his craft of tentmaking so as not to be dependent upon the churches for his daily living expenses.[39] Bivocational ministry permits relatively inexpensive expansion of the church into new areas and frees up funds for ministry that would have otherwise been designated for salaries. It does, however, impose constraints

37. The first book in this literature was published eighty years ago—Barton, *The Man Nobody Knows*—which was an exposition of Jesus as a business leader. A more recent version of this is Jones, *Jesus CEO*.

38. It is interesting to observe the plethora and variety of professional ministry titles available today. No longer are the choices confined to deacon, Christian education, music, children, and youth. There are ministers of small groups, worship arts, media, spiritual formation, discipleship, ethnic-specific ministries, gender-specific ministries, administration, program development, entrepreneurship, etc. The Church continues to be very creative.

39. Bickers, *The Tentmaking Pastor*.

of time and access upon those who would seek to serve in this role; if the dominant paradigm is not concurrently challenged, it is easy to burn out in this model.[40]

Third, many of those who are called or directed to professional ministry end up practicing within the context of the parachurch organization. It is unclear yet whether the parachurch represents a temporary aberration in American religious history, a response to the church's own inadequacies in fulfilling its mission, or whether the parachurch will, in the long run, represent another of those new "denominational" alignments of the twenty-first century. Parachurches do have the advantage of crossing denominational lines, via the support of denominational institutions or their members, and thus are not usually as guilty of the identity exclusion noted earlier for traditional denominations. And they are often more flexible in terms of who they will utilize in ministry, ordination or other such credentials not normally being necessary for their professional roles.[41] This, of course, presents its own problems.

A fourth response to the dilemma of cultural expectations has been the rediscovery of the five-fold ministry model portrayed in Ephesians 4. Frost and Hirsch identify this model by the acronym "APEPT" (Apostle, Prophet, Evangelist, Pastor, and Teacher).[42] The house church movement has also tapped into this model as a biblical and practical method to provide leadership to small groups that must, almost by definition, be led by laity. This model has the advantages of definition by gifting, rather than cultural function, and of leading via teams, rather than by solo efforts. Teaming is a popular phenomenon in the management disciplines today, but it also appeals to the desire for relational structures.

The issue of ministerial credentialing is another with which the American church has not yet fully grappled, in light of the changes summarized above. If one practices ordination, to what is

---

40. See Kreider et al., *New House Church Networks.* I know something of this because of personal experience as a bivocational minister since 1994.

41. Willmer, *The Prospering Parachurch.*

42. Frost and Hirsch, *The Shaping of Things to Come,* 165–81.

one ordained? Many denominations ordained only for the pastor-ate, but it is growing increasingly difficult to define what constitutes "the pastorate," given the multitude of roles and functions available within the church. The denomination with which this author is affiliated typically ordains only senior pastors, although a separate ordination track for chaplains (a track that disqualifies them from the pastorate) has recently been created. Other professional ministers are invited to pursue a "specialized ministries license," which is a catchall category on a non-ordination track.[43] These distinctions are becoming increasingly untenable, both in practice and in theology. We need a Protestant theology of ordination for the twenty-first century.

The American church is apparently undergoing another wave of democratization, similar in some respects to that which propelled the Baptists and Methodists to the forefront of American religion in the early decades of the nineteenth century. There is growing impatience with the wall of separation between laity and clergy and increasing efforts to unleash the power of the laity. There is no doubt that leadership is necessary in these efforts; the forms that such leadership will take, however, may grow more radical in the decades to come.

THE LONG WAY: A PRELIMINARY GLIMPSE AT THE DESTINATIONS

This chapter has reviewed three possible destinations for the twenty-first century church, each involving new definitions or understandings. Our new definition of church will introduce models to the Western world that are either new or revivals of ancient ideas. Our new understanding of denominationalism may have the potential to move us from exclusive, institutional forms to more inclusive, relational networks. And our new definition of profes-

43. "Pastoral Ministry Handbook." Huntington, IN: Church of the United Brethren in Christ, 2009. http://www.ub.org/ministers/PMHandbook/04 SpecialMinisters.html.

sional ministry may result in a fresh theology of ordination and the unleashing of the power of the laity within the new church.

Seth Godin is a professional marketer who has given us the concept of the "ideavirus" and, more recently, the image of the "purple cow."[44] A purple cow is something remarkable, noteworthy, something that provokes the kind of attention and reaction that a purple cow would in a herd of black and white heifers. While Godin writes for businesses, his call for purple cows is appropriate to the Church as well, even as the motivation is different. The Church has often fallen prey to the novelty of the new and different, particularly in its hyper-attractional phases, but this is hardly a problem in which the Church and its message are increasingly perceived as irrelevant at best and downright intolerant at worst. Because the models of congregational life, denominational relationships, and professional ministry expectations are so thoroughly culture-bound, it has been difficult to free the Church from the dominant paradigms in all three contexts. But it must happen.

The good news is that the dominant cultural paradigm need not be replaced by another dominant model. This chapter began with an analogy of pilgrims on a journey to multiple destinations, most of which are mile markers on the way to our ultimate rest. These destinations are indeed plural; one model will no longer suffice. Some may choose to stop at one place and another somewhere else. Should we be able to affirm one another in such choices and resist the temptation to erect exclusionary barriers against one another at the time of such choices, the American Church may at least achieve some measure of unity of mission amidst a bewildering plurality of forms. And, if so, it may likewise be able to achieve some measure of unity of mission with the education institutions to which it has given birth.

44. Godin, *Purple Cow*. See also his *Unleashing the Ideavirus*, which is similar in some respects to Malcolm Gladwell's more familiar *The Tipping Point*.

4

Metaphors for the Academy's Journey

WALKING THE WAY OF METAPHOR

> Metaphor is a tool so ordinary that we use it unconsciously and automatically, with so little effort that we hardly notice it. It is omnipresent: metaphor suffuses our thoughts, no matter what we are thinking about. It is accessible to everyone: as children, we automatically, as a matter of course, acquire a mastery of everyday metaphor. It is conventional: metaphor is an integral part of our ordinary everyday thought and language. And it is irreplaceable: metaphor allows us to understand our selves [sic] and our world in way that no other modes of thought can.[1]

MARK TURNER and George Lakoff follow this paean to the metaphor with this observation: "Far from being a matter of words, metaphor is a matter of thought. . . . It is indispensable not only to our imagination but also to our reason."[2] It is the importance of metaphor to our imaginations that is of importance here. If, in fact, as James Lawley and Penny Tompkins argue, metaphor is the language of our internal realities, then it is the means by which we perceive the world and communicate such

1. Lakoff and Turner, *More Than Cool Reason*, xi.
2. Ibid.

perceptions to ourselves and others.[3] In short, we create our own realities through the metaphors that we employ.

This concept is not so startling as it first appears. Lawley and Tompkins have combined this idea of metaphoric construction of reality with David Grove's methodology of clean language to create a therapeutic model called "symbolic modelling [sic]."[4] The therapist employs Symbolic Modelling to explore metaphors (symbols) as a means of understanding how the individual perceives his/her reality. Thus, debilitating images of one's self or one's situation can be articulated, claimed, and addressed. The clean language philosophy, however, resists the introduction of new metaphors into the imagination of the client, as this would "dirty" the conversation with the metaphors of the interviewer. Metaphors must be owned by and original to the user.

Therapeutic concerns aside, introducing new metaphors into the conversation may indeed be the best way to change realities, either one's own or those of others. Howard Gardner, the noted educational theorist who introduced the concept of multiple intelligences, has argued that the process of changing minds is that of changing "mental representations," a concept similar to that of "symbolic models."[5] If the language one utilizes is capable of changing one's reality, then the introduction and appropriation of new language, new symbols, and new metaphors into the conversation may result in a change of perception by the other. This understanding of the role of language is derived from the later thought of Ludwig Wittgenstein, who explored the power of language to organize and articulate ideas. Gardner describes it such: "Later Wittgensteins saw language as creating the cognitive worlds in which we are enmeshed."[6]

---

3. Lawley and Tompkins, *Metaphors in Mind*, 3.

4. Grove and Panzer, *Resolving Traumatic Memories*.

5. Gardner, *Changing Minds*, 7. Gardner's methods of changing mental representations are reason, research, resonance, representational redescriptions, resources and rewards, real world events, and resistances (15–18).

6. Ibid., 191.

The purpose of this introductory exploration of the power of metaphor is to frame the discussion that follows. It is, perhaps, to use the metaphor of "metaphor" as a means of understanding the historic conversations and relationships between church and academy in the United States, which is the topic of this chapter. It is to suggest that the relationships between church and academy have been understood by different parties primarily through a series of competing metaphors. It is to argue that these metaphors have both explanatory power and boundary-setting limitations. And it is to suggest that new metaphors (maybe even new categories of metaphors) may be necessary to create new realities and new relationships in the twenty-first century.

THE FIRST CATEGORY:
METAPHORS OF RELATIONSHIP

The narrative of Christian higher education in the United States has long been dominated by a myth of declension, the chief metaphor of which is the "slippery slope." Perhaps first articulated by William Buckley's provocative *God and Man at Yale* in 1951,[7] which chastised the title university for its offhanded or combative attitude toward religion, it received its most comprehensive and controversial treatment in James Burtchaell's *The Dying of the Light*,[8] the very title of which contains a powerful metaphor of the myth of declension. The pungency of Burtchaell's work lies in his choice of narratives. Rather than looking like Buckley to the schools of the Ivy League, which by the end of the twentieth century had long before been written off by the fundamentalist-evangelical wing of American Christianity, Burtchaell turned his attention to 17 smaller colleges and universities, most of whom still considered themselves in some way "Christian."[9]

7. Buckley, *God and Man at Yale*.

8. Burtchaell, *The Dying of the Light*. The subtitle ("The Disengagement of Colleges and Universities from Their Christian Churches") indicates which party Burtchaell held responsible for the "dying of the light."

9. The schools and the denominational families they represented were as

His argument was that the connections between church and academy had weakened in the twentieth century, that this weakening had nearly universal application, including colleges that considered themselves immune, and that a variety of forces were responsible for this phenomenon. In particular, he blames rationalism and pietism for separating academic life from religious life, and ultimately marginalizing religion as a voluntary expression of personal spirituality without inherent linkage to the core pursuit of knowledge that was the mission of the American university. He likewise distributes the blame among the leaders of both church and academy (although it is obvious that he lays the majority of the burden at the feet of university leaders). All were complicit in the "alienation" of the academy from the church; all acquiesced to external pressures, whether from accrediting bodies or other sorts of pressure, to modify the faith mission of the Christian college.

Burtchaell is particularly scathing in his attack on the perceived gap between the rhetoric and behavior of the institutions. In one paragraph of rather heated prose, he expounds:

> This degraded rhetoric in which both colleges and churches have indulged is more delusional than deceitful. It bespeaks an ardent conviction that the colleges' educational purposes have remained the same, only now they are being pursued more sagaciously. Those who speak this way are being beguiled more than anyone who cares to listen. Both educators and church officers have been persuaded that their churches have no intellectual insight or critical gift that would distinguish them as academic mentors. To sidestep embarrassment they must reduce their description of the colleges' ambitions and churches' expectations to secular bafflegab. This strange discourse deserves a Pascal to describe it, for it has been providing the background music to distract everyone but cantankerous critics from watching the critical swerve from pietism

---

follows: Dartmouth and Beliot (Congregationalist); Lafayette and Davidson (Presbyterian); Millsaps and Ohio Wesleyan (Methodist); Wake Forest, Virginia Union, and Linfield (Baptist); Gettysburg, St. Olaf, and Concordia (Lutheran); Boston College, New Rochelle, St. Mary's College of California (Catholic); and Azusa Pacific and Dordt (Evangelical).

directly into indifferentism and then into the academic vari-
ant of rationalism.[10]

The reaction, of course, was strong.

Some of the reaction was due to the intentional similarities between Burtchaell's work and the less controversial, more
celebrated work of George Marsden four years earlier.[11] Like
Burtchaell, Marsden expounded a myth of declension and, like
Burtchaell, Marsden illustrated his theory by exploring the historical narratives of a variety of American colleges and universities that (once) had some sort of explicit faith connection.[12] But
Marsden's metaphors are a bit different, although perhaps no less
provocative. Picking up on Buckley's then four-decade-old thesis,
he explored the concept of "losing one's soul." His argument is that
these dominant American universities sacrificed their faith-based
identities in the late nineteenth and earlier twentieth centuries
through the agency of liberal Protestantism, which increasingly
viewed its own agenda as synonymous with that of the American
nation. The irony of that position, Marsden notes, is that the identification with American national culture became, over time, more
pronounced in these universities than their identification with the
faith communities they believed had given rise to that culture.
Religious life was thus marginalized in the name of religious establishment. They had lost their soul.

Marsden's thesis is compelling, both because of its rigorous
historical analysis and because his tone is rational and evenhanded.
Less compelling is the argument of one who was a major player in
many of the decisions that led to the growing distance between a
number of these colleges and the churches with which they were
related. Merrimon Cuninggim was a graduate of, leader in, or
observer of a number of the schools discussed by Burtchaell and
Marsden, or schools similar to them. He takes umbrage at the myth

10. Ibid., 850.

11. Marsden, *The Soul of the American University*.

12. Marsden's subjects included Yale, Michigan, Cornell, California, Johns
Hopkins, Harvard, Princeton, and Chicago.

of declension, expressed either as "slippery slope" or "losing one's soul," and proposes instead the metaphor of "uneasy partners." He acknowledges that church and college experienced considerable difficulties in maintaining relationships in the twentieth century, but is optimistic that such relationships can be maintained or even enhanced within the new realities.[13]

His proposals for doing so, however, strike one as either naïve or simplistic. In his discussion of the "archetype" of a "church-related college" (his preferred descriptor), he suggests three "requisites" for such a relationship:

1. "A church-related college must possess a sense of its past, its rootage, and must show by its life—that is, by both its professions and its practices—that is has a lively appreciation of its history and present character."[14]

2. "A church-related college must have an understanding of, and must practice, the essential academic values."[15]

3. "A church-related college must have a relationship with a church...that is credible and mutually understood."[16]

Given his illustrations, apparently, the college can affirm its history and make a few symbolic gestures toward the church with which it is connected, provided such gestures do not interfere with its primary academic mission or "values," which are indistinguishable from those of colleges that do not possess such a connection. The institution is thus "church-related" but not "faith-based" (a

---

13. Cuninggim, *Uneasy Partners*. Cuninggim writes after the publication of Marsden's book but before that of Burtchaell. However, both of them had first made public their theses in Neuhaus's periodical *First Things*, prior to the publication of their monographs, so Cuninggim was familiar with their arguments. See Burtchaell, "The Decline and Fall of the Christian College," 16–29; and "The Decline and Fall of the Christian College (II)," 30–38; and Marsden, "The Soul of the American University," 34–47. Marsden had also co-edited a volume with Brad Longfield entitled *The Secularization of the Academy*.

14. Cuninggim, *Uneasy Partners*, 99.

15. Ibid., 102.

16. Ibid., 114.

term Cuninggim refuses to use). In fact, Cuninggim is particularly concerned that the church (which he views as a very potential
threat to autonomy) not interfere with the essential functions of the
college, which he perceives as neutral, universal, and cognitive.[17]
His compilation of over 750 church-related colleges in the United
States reveals his rather broad definition of "church-related" and
perhaps illustrates the thesis of Marsden and Burtchaell in ways he
did not anticipate.[18]

   A fourth metaphor (to lay alongside of "slippery slope," "losing one's soul," and "uneasy partners") provides a more positive
image. Richard Hughes and William Adrian used the term "contribution" to describe the relationship between certain theological or ecclesiastical traditions and the institutions they founded.[19]
Like Marsden and Burtchaell, they utilize narrative case studies
of specific institutions to illustrate their argument,[20] which is that
each theological tradition has something to contribute to the academic life and mission of the institutions that remain within that
tradition. There is no single model of Christian higher education;
they offer multiple models that reflect the distinctives of particular traditions. Thus, while not explicitly contradicting the myth

17   "A college is an educational institution with a sharp set of purposes
for its clientele—to inform their minds with the best that has been produced
in those fields of substance significant for the world's work, to encourage the
mind to understand that substance and that work, and to foster the ability to
express to others much of what is learned and understood" (Ibid., 96).

18. His list includes such dubious entries as Lebanon Valley College,
Elizabethtown College, Wilson College, and Franklin and Marshall College,
all central Pennsylvania institutions with which I have personal knowledge.
None are identified in the public mind with a church or any kind of explicit
faith commitment. Ibid., 126–47.

19. Hughes and Adrian, *Models for Christian Higher Education.*

20. Their representative institutions and their founding faith communities are the College of St. Benedict/St. John's University and the University
of Portland (Roman Catholic), St. Olaf and California Lutheran (Lutheran),
Calvin and Whitworth (Reformed), Goshen and Fresno Pacific (Mennonite),
Wheaton and Seattle Pacific (Evangelical/Interdenominational), Messiah
and Point Loma Nazarene (Wesleyan/Holiness), Samford (Baptist), and
Pepperdine (Restorationist).

of declension, they are nevertheless presenting an optimistic understanding of the relationship between church and academy that does not depend on the abrogation of faith-based distinctives on the part of the academy.[21]

These four metaphors have guided the discussions thus far; perhaps there is room for one or more new guiding metaphors for the twenty-first century. This book uses the words "connection" and "collaboration" as two admittedly vague offerings. Others will surely be generated as the discussion continues.

THE SECOND CATEGORY:
METAPHORS OF FAITH AND LEARNING

In addition to the metaphors of institutional relationship, Christian scholars and administrators have exerted considerable energy creating and exploring metaphors to describe the interactions between faith and learning in the academy. In their historical narrative of Wheaton College in the Hughes and Adrian text, Michael Hamilton and James Mathisen present four models of these interactions as they have been played out at Wheaton over the past century and a half.[22] Since Wheaton has been a significant player in the historical development of the dominant models, these four models (or metaphors) provide a useful template for this discussion.

The "convergence model," popular in the nineteenth century, perceived no distinction or conflict between knowledge received through revelation and that received through other epistemologies. Built upon the "natural theology" of William Paley and Joseph Butler,[23] it assumed a unity of knowledge (and of knowing), that "the system of discovered (or natural) knowledge and the system of revealed (or divine) knowledge are thought to be

---

21. Their work has been supported by Benne, *Quality with Soul*.

22. Hamilton and Mathisen, "Faith and Learning at Wheaton College," 268–71.

23. Paley, *Natural Theology*; Butler, *The Analogy of Religion*.

complete in themselves, yet mutually confirming."[24] It received its fullest expression in John Cardinal Neumann's *The Idea of a University.*[25] Interestingly, some of the proponents of the "intelligent design" movement resurrected natural theology in the late twentieth century as a philosophical foundation for their ideas, [26] but for most Christian scholars the notion of the unity of truth has been replaced by one of the dichotomous models discussed below or a more ambiguous postmodern model of multiple truths.

The "triumphalist model" resulted from what Hamilton and Mathisen term "the shattering of the nineteenth-century synthesis of faith and learning."[27] In the "highly-polarized" setting that resulted from the rise of Darwinism and higher criticism, this triumphalism took both secular and Christian forms, as proponents on both sides of the divide sought to discredit the truth claims of the other. It was triumphalism that led to the fundamentalist movement of the early twentieth century (and the schools that were founded by that movement) and to the marginalization of Christianity in the formerly Christian institutions of the Ivy League. Both forms of this model are still evident in the rhetoric of some extremists in each camp—in Bible institutions that do not admit "secular learning" and in some private or state-sponsored institutions that are antithetical to the inclusion of religion in academic life except, perhaps, as sociology or literature.

The "values-added model" is also known as the "separate spheres" model and is a dominant metaphor in many church-related institutions. "It assumes that secular knowledge and sacred knowledge do not conflict because they occupy different spheres. The two kinds of knowledge do not change each other in fundamental ways, but they can enrich each other."[28] In this model, there is a single, universal methodology employed by mathematicians,

24. Hamilton and Mathisen, "Faith and Learning at Wheaton College," 268.

25. Neumann, *The Idea of a University.*

26. Johnson, *The Wedge of Truth.*

27. Hamilton and Mathisen, "Faith and Learning at Wheaton College," 269.

28. Ibid., 270.

for instance, irrespective of whatever faith commitments they may possess. If anything, one's faith commitment "adds to" one's work as a mathematician by providing a veneer of values that may (or may not) be missing otherwise. In the academy, the "values-added" approach regards learning as a neutral activity that is indistinguishable from one environment to another, and one's faith commitment is played out in "sacred" activities, such as chapel services, missions or service projects, personal relationships, and other non-academic activities, which are regarded as supplements to the core academic mission.

The fourth metaphor, which was originally developed at Wheaton by philosopher Arthur Holmes, is the "integration model."[29] Holmes begins with the assumption that all scholars bring certain presuppositions to their scholarly work and that therefore there is no such thing as "neutral" inquiry. If one brings secular assumptions to the scholarly task, the outcomes of that work will be distorted in that direction. If, however, one begins with Christian foundations, then both the methodology and the outcomes of scholarly endeavor will reflect the scholar's faith commitment.[30] One's faith, then, consists of a collection of assumptions and faith statements that are expected to inform both the theory and practice of one's discipline. The practical manifestation of this metaphor was the creation of the "faith integration paper" at Calvin College in the 1980s and since then adopted by a number of other colleges and universities, particularly those associated with the Council of Christian Colleges and Universities, as a demonstration of the faculty member's ability to integrate at sufficient depth.

The "integration model" has become the dominant metaphor for evangelical institutions and the scholars they employ. It has received support from numerous points, explicitly so from the likes of Nicholas Wolterstorff, whose *Reason within the Bounds of Religion* explored the role of belief in choosing between competing theories in the academy, and George Marsden, whose *The*

---

29. See Holmes, *All Truth is God's Truth* and *The Idea of a Christian College*.

30. Hamilton and Mathisen, "Faith and Learning at Wheaton College," 271.

Outrageous Idea of Christian Scholarship used Holmes as a starting point to make a creative argument for Christian scholarship from the vantage point of "perspectivalism": If multiple cultures and voices are to be heard in the academy, then the Christian "voice" needs to be invited into the conversation as well.[31] And implicit if indirect support has been given by the deconstructionist movement, which demolished the "neutrality myth" of "objective scholarship" and has inadvertently made room for distinct rationalities inherent within faith communities.[32]

Both the "values added" and "integration" models have come under increased scrutiny in the past decade, primarily because of their insistence on distinguishing between "faith" and "learning" as distinct entities that should or should not be "mixed" or "integrated." While recognizing that these models have merit, there have been efforts to produce other metaphors for Christian scholarship, particularly for scholars who do not intentionally reside within the Reformed tradition from which the integration model was birthed. Douglas and Rhonda Jacobsen call for "enlarging the conversation" to include other traditions and other models, particularly those explicated by the other contributors to the volume.[33] A 2004 conference sponsored by the Jacobsens, "Faith and the Academy," provided further exposition and illustration of these additional metaphors.[34]

Crystal Downing offers an interesting metaphor—imbrication—as a fresh contribution to the discussion of the relationship between faith and learning. She rejects integration as reflecting

31. Wolterstorff, *Reason within the Bounds of Religion*; Marsden, *The Outrageous Idea of Christian Scholarship*.

32. See Derrida, *A Derrida Reader*; Alasdair MacIntyre, *Whose Justice?*

33. Jacobsen and Jacobsen, *Scholarship and Christian Faith*. Contributors included colleagues of the Jacobsens at Messiah College—Rodney Sawatsky, Crystal Downing, Edward Davis, David Weaver-Zercher, Susanna Bede Caroselli, and Kim Phipps. See particularly Sawatsky's chapter on "The Virtue of Scholarly Hope," which includes an argument for "hope" against the myth of declension.

34. "Faith in the Academy," September 30–October 2, 2004, Messiah College, Grantham, Pennsylvania.

"modernist sensibilities, valorizing the autonomy of the individual, who within himself melds faith and scholarship into a unified, almost monumental form—like modernist architecture."[35] Using architecture as her paradigm, she promotes imbrication, which evokes the image of overlapping shingles on a roof, as a worthy postmodern metaphor of humility, one that "registers awareness that we are made up of multiple vocabularies, some of which overlap, others of which do not, but all of which are manifestations of the self."[36] Imbrication is less tidy, methodologically, than integration but is perhaps more reflective of the realities of academic life, in which some things are integrated, many are not, and one learns to live, at least temporarily, with dichotomies, trichotomies, and "multiplichotomies" that are part of the messiness of postmodern scholarship.

Susanna Bede Caroselli uses the discipline of art history to extrapolate the notions of "considered response," the analytical imagination with which one typically identifies scholarship), and "instinctive response," the emotional reaction that scholars are expected to suppress. Using a late fifteenth century Florentine altarpiece as an example, she pleads that "a general conclusion about the didactic, penitential nature of this image might be reached through disinterested scholarship (considered response); it is also accessible through instinctive response alone. But a synthesis of the two approaches yields a richer and more resonant result, and the one that allows the scholars to comprehend better, if not experience, the intended effect of this image on its original viewers . . ."[37] Caroselli fails to explain how this dual epistemology reflects a blending of faith and learning; in fact, she argues the obvious point that instinctive response is not limited to Christians. It will require additional reflection to determine if there is a response (similar to or beyond "instinctive") that persons of faith bring to scholarship

35. Downing, "Imbricating Faith and Learning," in Jacobsen and Jacobsen, 40.

36. Ibid., 41.

37. Caroselli, "Instinctive Response as a Tool for the Scholar," 145.

and that has potential for unpacking meanings not visible to those who do not see through that lens.

The metaphors of "imbrication" and "instinct" are newly introduced and have not been developed as fully as the "integration" metaphor. Like it, they have limitations of their own. Alongside of these metaphors are those of various faith traditions, as discussed in both the Jacobsen and Jacobsen text and the Hughes and Adrian study. These include the peacemaking and service motifs of the Anabaptist tradition, in which scholarship is inherently more oriented to praxis than to mere analysis; the social ethics theme of the Roman Catholic tradition, in which the Thomistic concept of the unity of knowledge is still preserved in some contexts; and the Lutheran tradition, in which the "separate spheres" language is native to the tradition (and for which, therefore, the integration model has presented a significant challenge, the metaphor being in contradiction to essential Lutheran understandings).

Other writers have begun to explore unique disciplinary aspects of the interaction between faith and learning. For instance, Edward Davis' essay examines the relationship between science and faith, and how historians of science in particular are abandoning the "warfare" metaphor for something that could best be described as dialogue.[38] And it is obvious to even the ardent integrationist that the faith of the scholar has a different "feel" or "look" when the scholar is a mathematician than when the scholar is an anthropologist. Even in an interdisciplinary era, the methodological assumptions that distinguish the natural sciences from the social sciences and both from the humanities will likely be increasingly reflected in how Christians understand the role of faith in their scholarship.

THE WAY OF METAPHOR: CAN WE HAVE SOME MORE?

The anti-intellectualism that is latent or explicit in much of American evangelicalism probably has its roots in the triumphalism of the

---

38. Davis, "Is There a Christian History of Science?" 63–76.

late nineteenth century.[39] The "scandal of the evangelical mind," as expressed by Mark Noll and others,[40] is not likely to disappear as long as evangelicalism as a tradition continues. However, there is counter-balancing scandal of the liberal Protestant mind, at least as far as Marsden and others have explicated it. The selling-out of liberal Protestantism to American nationalism in the early twentieth century has now been replaced by a selling-out to multicultural relativism of the modernist variety.

Therefore, both evangelicalism and liberalism need fresh incentives to engage in critical, creative scholarship that bears the distinctive mark of a vibrant Christian faith—scholarship that is not just about Christianity or the church but scholarship by public believers about everything scholars study. This new scholarship will draw freely upon all Christian traditions, including those that have hitherto been largely ignored by Protestants in particular, and upon all "secularized" disciplines to create interdisciplinary studies with fresh visions of the living out of Christian faith.

For example, the "faith integration paper" required for tenure at many evangelical Christian universities is likely to be replaced by something that provides multiple means to articulate and demonstrate how one's faith impacts one's life as a scholar-practitioner. This writer was a member of the committee that evaluates the faith integration papers at his institution. The members of that committee hold the careers of their colleagues in their hands: a faculty member whose paper is not approved is not granted tenure but is instead offered a one-year terminal contract before dismissal. Multiple means of demonstration may allow those to succeed who are capable of expressing their faith in their actions as a scholar in forms other than the fairly rigid straitjacket of the assignment as currently constructed.

If the creation or appropriation of metaphors creates our realities or "mental representations," then the new metaphors that are intruding into the conversations discussed in this chapter will

39. Douglas John Hall noted that this triumphalism affected their understanding of the atonement as well. Hall, *The Cross in our Context.*

40. Noll, *The Scandal of the Evangelical Mind.*

certainly alter both the tone and the content of those conversations. As the Jacobsens have argued, there is a need to "enlarge the conversation." This metaphor implies both an invitation for others who have hitherto been excluded to join the discussion and a willingness to explore topics that have been left by the wayside during the two overlapping and long-enduring conversations noted herein—the relationship between church and academy and the relationship between faith and learning. And perhaps there is even opportunity to reframe these two conversations, so that the motifs of secularism, declension, and integration are someday no longer dominant.

The postmodern academy and the postmodern church are likely to be much more comfortable than their modernist counterparts with the ambiguities inherent in these relationships. If "faith" is someday no longer perceived in the academy as cognitive content but the living out of one's relationship with God and His People; if the life of the mind can be remarried to the life of the spirit in a holistic theory of personhood; if static understandings of knowledge are replaced by developmental, even pilgrimage, models; and if the "silo" metaphor of the disciplines is supplanted by a "toolbox" or other similar metaphor—if all of these transitions already in progress become the hallmarks of the twenty-first century Christian academy, then new metaphors will need to be created, introduced, championed, and nurtured.

The forms of both church and academy have been largely unaltered throughout American history; the changes have been modifications on a theme, not expressions of new forms. New forms of both institutions are probably necessary in the twenty-first century, and these new forms are likely to provide fresh opportunities for collaborative relationships. This presents an opportunity for those who envision a greater level of collaboration. New metaphors are needed. No one model is likely to ever achieve the kind of dominance that some enjoyed at the end of the twentieth century; multiplicity of models will be the defining characteristic of the new century. Yet "multiplicity" is itself a metaphor and one that is likely to enjoy greater authority and credibility in the decades ahead. And it, like the others already on the table and the ones yet to be offered there, has the potential to create fresh pictures in the imaginations of the next generation of Christians in both the church and the academy.

5

Revolutions on the Academy's Journey

WALKING THE WAY OF REVOLUTION

WITHIN THE past fifteen years Western institutions of higher education have experienced multiple, simultaneous, intertwined revolutions to a degree not experienced since the founding of the first universities in the high middle ages.[1] In that initial revolution the cathedral schools morphed into degree-granting institutions with professional scholars, paying students, established curricula, and an administrative structure not entirely separate from but also not directly controlled by the Church. Later changes ("revolutions" may be too strong a word for these) saw the expansion of academic disciplines beyond the *trivium* and *quadrivium*,

---

1. The use of the word "revolutions" here, while seemingly hyperbolic, is actually derived from another source written a full decade ago: "A revolution…has been slowly unfolding during the past several decades transforming the landscape of higher education, not only here in the United States but also throughout the world. This transformation in education is often referred to as the 'Adult Student Revolution.' Sparked by social, cultural, economic and technological factors, this sea-change is rightly called a "revolution" since it is causing astute educators, like scientists undergoing a paradigm shift, to assume pioneering attitudes and adopt unprecedented methods which the influx of adult students onto college campuses demands." See Naugle, "The Christian College and Adult Education," 24–25.

65

the beginnings of state-sponsored lower and higher education, the creation and ascendance of the Doctor of Philosophy degree for professional scholars, the secularization of the academy (discussed in Chapter 4) and the consequent birth of the Bible college movement, and, most recently, the politicization and commercialization of the American university.[2] Each of these has exerted a powerful influence on the nature and character of higher education in the early twenty-first century, yet this chapter argues that there are other revolutions that have the potential to entirely remake and redefine higher education in the quarter century ahead, and that such remaking and redefining may not necessarily be a bad thing.

THE FIRST REVOLUTION: ADULT EDUCATION

As indicated, the revolutions are multiple and intertwined but may be defined as consisting of four distinct strands. The first is a revolution in adult education, during which the number of "non-traditional students" (variously defined as age twenty-two and over or twenty-five and over) in formal higher education programs increased from a miniscule fraction of the total enrollment in the 1980s to a *majority* of total college and university enrollment in the United States in the early twenty-first century.[3] Indeed, it is

2. Each of these changes has generated its own spate of literature, with the politicization of the university and its supposed commercialization creating the most recent round. Among the best in the latter category is Derek Bok's *Universities in the Marketplace*, both because of his credentials as a former president of Harvard University and because of a tone more reasoned than that some of the other texts on the topic. See also Hersh and Merrow, *Declining By Degrees*, which is a companion book to a PBS series quite critical of the state of American higher education.

3. "Between 1970 and 1985, the United States saw a 115% rise in adult students entering college. Since 1985, this increase has continued until now more than 50% of the undergraduate student body on many campuses is comprised of adult students (students over 25 years old)" (Fidler, "Teaching Adult Students"). Or, put another way, of the 15 million or so college and university students in the United States in 2005, only about 45 percent were the "traditional age" of eighteen to twenty-two, and the median age of all students is twenty-nine (Hersh and Merrow, *Declining by Degrees*, 1).

appropriate to argue that while higher education programs for adult students may be yet "non-traditional," it is certainly "mainstream." This revolution was fueled by the pioneering work of Malcolm Knowles[4] in the 1970s and enhanced by significant theoretical and empirical studies ever since, to the point where "andragogy" is increasingly distinguished from "pedagogy" in operational terms (or even where pedagogical principles are being refined and revised to include some basic andragogical principles).

Typical of andragogical principles is the understanding of the role of the instructor as a "facilitator" of learning, rather than merely as the repository, transmitter, or conduit of knowledge. Traditional pedagogy[5] is still somewhat Lockean in its orientation (although this is seldom admitted), in that the student is perceived, at least in part, as a *tabula rasa* upon which can be written or drawn what is known about a particular discipline. The instructor is the chief chalk artist.[6] In Knowles' understanding, however, the adult student has accomplished considerable learning before coming to the classroom. This learning may be application in search of theory, or the reverse; both are situations in which a facilitator of learning can help the student make connections. Further, in andragogy students learn from each other; learning is multidirectional, multilateral, and multiphased, all of which requires someone to facilitate and capture the learning experience.

The "learning experience" is a familiar phrase in andragogy, due largely to the work of David Kolb[7] and others in creating a model by which experiential learning can be captured, evaluated,

4. Knowles, *The Modern Practice of Adult Education*; and Knowles, *The Adult Learner*.

5. The word "traditional" is used here quite intentionally, as a younger generation of teachers is imbibing freely from andragogical theory and other, more postmodern, understandings of the learning process; the characterization here as "chalk artist" would not do them justice.

6. This is, of course, a highly generalized and colloquial presentation of John Locke's philosophy of education as presented in *An Essay Concerning Human Understanding*.

7. Kolb, *Experiential Learning*.

and encouraged. Drawing on the work of John Dewey[8], Kolb has developed both his eponymous model and a "learning style inventory" that seeks to locate each student's learning style on a point in his cycle of experiential learning. Regardless of the models and inventories, the use of experiential learning techniques, both to evaluate prior learning and to encourage future learning, has challenged or changed fundamental assumptions about the acquisition of knowledge, the learning process, and the relationship between knowledge and learning, particularly among adults.

THE SECOND REVOLUTION: NEW DELIVERIES

If the first revolution is addressed to a particular demographic group, the second revolution has provided a delivery structure and philosophy that provided access to these students. Even those institutions of higher learning that had adopted a congenial approach to the adult student (through re-entry programs, for example)[9] had not necessarily made their educational offerings more accessible to those with career and family responsibilities. Previous to the 1980s "adult education" consisted largely of non-credit or non-degreed courses in job training or skills development for employment or in recreational learning (e.g. arts for the senior citizen or homemaker). If one wanted for-credit courses or a degree, one would have to attend courses at a college campus with traditional-aged students during the day, and thus either quit one's job to do so full-time or find jobs that could accommodate this schedule.

Then in the 1980s one began to see a proliferation of for-credit programs offered through evening and weekend classes, primarily through "continuing education" or "extension" units within the

8. Dewey, *Experience and Education.*

9. For a first-person account of utilizing such programs as an adult student, see Fungaroli, *Traditional Degrees for Nontraditional Students.* Fungaroli seems oblivious, however, to the other aspects of the adult student revolution; despite its publishing date of 2000, it appears to have been written in the 1980s.

colleges and universities.[10] These finally provided opportunities for adult students to earn a degree, albeit with considerable sacrifice or patience. One of my relatives earned his associate's degree at a community college after ten years of taking one course a semester. The other option, observed by this author while teaching in such programs in the 1990s, was for the student to take up to three courses a semester, which meant three evenings a week away from home in class and many more hours of study during the other evenings and weekends. Even at this pace, it could take a decade to earn a bachelor's degree.

Finally, in the early 1990s[11] one began to see the growth of "accelerated programs" for working adults. These programs are based on two controversial premises: 1) that "seat time" is not, by itself, a sufficient measure of the quality of learning that takes place, and 2) that students are more likely to succeed if the learning takes place within a consistent and supportive social network known as a "cohort." Many of these programs were and are labeled "degree completion programs"[12] and were designed for adult students who had previously earned an associate's degree or its equivalent and need to complete their baccalaureate. A typical format consisted of creating a cohort of 10–14 students who would together take a

10. I had the opportunity to be a student in a program that was truly ahead of its time in the late 1980s. I enrolled in a Master of Christian Ministries program through the Graduate School for Christian Ministries at Huntington College in Huntington, Indiana (one of the three case study institutions in this volume). Courses were scheduled around three weeklong residencies each year, with pre-residency readings and assignments and a post-residency project completing the course requirements. Although I was living and working in Pennsylvania, I traveled to Indiana three times a year and completed the 34-credit program in two and a half years. This option no longer exists.

11. Eastern University, where I am employed, actually introduced its first accelerated program in 1989. It was the first in the Delaware Valley, which is, if anything, over-populated with institutions of higher education. Today there are two dozen other institutions in that adult market.

12. The ubiquitous search engine Google now inadvertently provides instant data for sociological analysis of cultural trends. A Google search for "degree completion program" results in over slightly less than 4 million hits (as of February, 2010), indicating something of the size of this market.

series of five-week courses in sequence, meeting one night a week for four hours.

The advantage to the student was the one-night-a-week classroom commitment, but the reduction in seat hours from traditional classrooms (20 hours instead of 40) meant that the student would be expected to participate in more individualized learning activities outside of class. Taking one class at a time allowed students to focus and taking the classes together as a cohort provided for retention rates that equaled or exceeded those of traditional programs. And the courses were increasingly offered at locations convenient to the student (perhaps even at her workplace) rather than solely on college campuses. The disadvantages to the student included the inflexibility of the program sequence (due to the desire to keep the cohort together), difficulties in meeting the eligibility requirements for financial aid programs, and the pace of the program (due to its accelerated nature).

THE THIRD REVOLUTION: PRACTITIONER FACULTY

To accommodate the large influx of students into these very popular programs, a third revolution took place. Higher education has been the domain of professional scholars for centuries and non-professionals (i.e., adjunct instructors) had been utilized only as a last resort (i.e., when financial limitations dictated that a full-time faculty member could not be available to teach a particular class). Even then, the preferred adjunct was a beginning scholar (someone in search of a full-time teaching position) or a retired scholar, and therefore to be regarded as at least somewhat professional. The new adult education programs in the 1990s, however, relied increasingly on non-professionals to teach their courses. These non-professionals were practitioners—individuals who had usually earned at least a master's degree (sometimes a doctorate) within their discipline but who preferred full-time practice in the workplace over full-time teaching or scholarship.[13]

13. Wachs, *The Case for Practitioner Faculty*.

The utilization of practitioners as adjunct, part-time faculty as the primary instructors in these programs had several effects. First, it permitted the professional studies programs (which represented the majority of the market) to provided "just-in-time" learning—to make applications from theory to the student's work context, to "teach you something you can take with you to work tomorrow and apply." The immediacy of such learning was attractive to adult students. Second, it permitted these programs to operate with a fairly high profit margin, which was almost a novel concept in higher education. Full-time, professional scholars are much more expensive than part-time instructors hired by the course. A handful of full-time faculty members (or, sometimes, none at all) would coordinate the academic components of programs that would utilize dozens, even hundreds, of adjunct practitioners. The downside to the use of practitioners as adjuncts, of course, was the expectation of serving as a "cash cow" for the rest of the university coupled with the perception or even reality of inferior academic quality.

The perception of inferior academic quality was met with a revolution in instructional design.[14] In fact, it may be argued that the discipline of instructional design, as applied to higher education, has grown out of the needs of adult programs to provide course materials for a new context. Very few faculty members in traditional programs of higher education take courses in pedagogy or instructional design; the expectation has been that those with a Ph.D. will have somehow learned to teach along the way. That this expectation has often not been justified is evident today in the number of faculty searches that require an instructional component and in the plethora of faculty development programs that are teaching faculty members how to teach.

Actual performance in the classroom is not the most significant challenge, however. Many faculty members are masterful communicators and know how to engage their students in the learning process. What they may not know how to do, however,

14. The dominant text in this newer discipline is Gagne et al., *Principles of Instructional Design*.

is to determine and achieve the ends toward which such learning should be directed. The professional teacher often encounters this need the first time he or she is asked to design a syllabus. The establishment of clearly articulated learning objectives, the design of learning activities (or "learning objects" or "lessons") that will accomplish those objectives while taking into account the varied learning styles and academic readiness of one's students, the choice of texts and other resources to support those learning activities, the choice of evaluative methods and criteria by which to determine if the learning objectives have been achieved, the very act of thinking of learning in such a fashion and acting upon that thinking—this is the essence of instructional design.

If full-time faculty members are lacking in basic instructional design principles, how can part-time adjunct practitioners be expected to apply these principles? In answer this question, creators of adult programs have often chosen to contract with others for the development of curriculum. The result has sometimes been called "modularized" curriculum and occasionally denigrated as "canned" curriculum. The process is different from school to school, but typically a "content expert" in a discipline works with a professional instructional designer to write a complete curriculum package for both students and instructors in a particular course. This permits the instructor to focus on facilitation of student learning and contextual application of theory rather than on the writing of lesson plans, the creation of tests and other evaluative instruments, and the choosing of texts. Those are all done for him by someone else.

The advantage to modularized curriculum is the opportunity for a practitioner to operate at a higher academic level than she would have likely been able to achieve, left to her own devices. It also provides for some consistency in the learning experience from one course to another and one cohort to another. The disadvantage is in the infrastructure necessary to write and continually revise such curriculum and to distribute it in a timely manner to both faculty and students. Modularized curriculum also limits the flexibility of an experienced instructor to choose texts, learning activities, or evaluative instruments in which he has more confidence or with which she has greater familiarity.[15] Full-time traditional faculty in universities that sponsor accelerated adult programs sometimes struggle with the curriculum in these programs as a result and sometimes even perform poorly on student or peer evaluations (usually to their great surprise).

THE FOURTH REVOLUTION: ONLINE LEARNING

There is one more revolutionary strand—the most controversial of them all—that has deeply impacted the nature of higher education in the past fifteen years, and that is the advent of online learning. On the one hand, online learning is merely the latest form of "distance education," which has been in existence in various forms for quite some time. On the other hand, online learning challenges some basic assumptions of the instructional task and the learning process, assumptions that have undergirded the academy for quite some time. Therefore, while for some online learning is yet another "delivery method," for others it is a threat to traditional understandings of the primacy of the instructor in the learning process and the means by which the transmission of knowledge occurs.

Online educational offerings grew quite naturally from the same forces that produced the one-night-a-week accelerated format for adult higher education and the mushrooming of off-campus classroom locations—the desire and demand for greater access to higher education. The progression is clear: the context of learning moves from the classroom to the boardroom to the bedroom (or the family room). Early attempts at online learning were mixed; without either experience or theory to provide direction, online education often degenerated into a poor-quality independent study or into a tragicomic farce as instructors attempted (vainly) to replicate their in-class methods for an online audience. Some who speak derogatively of online learning today remember

15. See Blair, "Best Practices," where I introduce the concept of "open source curriculum" as a third option between or beyond the syllabus and the modularized curriculum unit.

those experiences . . . and fail to acknowledge the changes in philosophy, methodology, and technology that have taken place even within the past five years.

Those committed to the cohort model of learning soon found ways to maintain some semblance of a relational culture online, and the major learning platforms (e.g., Blackboard and WebCT) brought together multiple technologies—email, synchronous discussion ("the chat room"), asynchronous discussion ("the discussion board"), audio, video streaming, database management, etc.—into a single dynamic environment that provides more flexibility for creative learning strategies than even many experienced online instructors have utilized. In today's market, the push to "go online" with one's academic offerings—particularly professional studies programs—is intense, both to respond to the aggressive actions of online competitors and to take advantage of the opportunity to increase one's enrollment (or, as the language of commerce is increasingly dominated this branch of higher education, one's "market share").

The criticisms of online learning are many and often heated. It is argued that online education reduces the role of the instructor, resulting in a lower quality of learning. Online learning does not take place within a community of learners, it is argued, and is therefore not to be recommended except to the most intrinsically motivated of students. It provides too many opportunities for academic dishonesty, as one does not know who is writing and submitting assignments. It frequently degenerates into insipid, forced online discussions where real learning does not take place. It limits the quantity and quality of interchange between student and instructor and between student and classmates. It is too technology-driven. And, finally, how one can learn without being in a classroom?

All of these criticisms are true . . . at times. And nearly every criticism here can be directed back at the traditional academic environment, the assumptions and practices of which have gone largely unchallenged for centuries because it was nearly the only model available. Now those assumptions and practices are being challenged as well[16] and the result is a fascinating discussion on contextualized educational strategies. Theory and empirical research are only now beginning to catch up. For the Christian university, these discussions have even more significant implications as they have (often for financial reasons) been among the most aggressive in promoting the revolutions described here. Besides, Christian universities have a theological commitment to their students that their secular counterparts do not share. It is entirely appropriate to ask if these revolutions further the mission of Christian higher education or whether they represent distractions from it. The remainder of this chapter addresses those concerns by articulating several fundamental assertions (labeled "resolutions") about human learning that, if true, can guide Christian institutions of higher learning through this revolutionary age.

THE WAY OF REVOLUTION: RESOLUTIONS FOR FUTURE WORLD-CHANGERS

This chapter has addressed four strands in a revolution in higher education in the West (particularly in the United States) over the past fifteen years. Those strands are 1) the large, unprecedented influx of adult students into institutions of higher learning, 2) the deliveries developed to provide access to these students, 3) the changes in teaching roles and instructional design as a result of these new deliveries, and 4) the proliferation of online programs. All four strands have created tensions, all have been controversial, and all are still new enough to be regarded by many as unwelcome intrusions into a previously calcified academic culture in the West. The following discussion introduces "resolutions" to help

16. For instance, those who protest the reduction (from traditional academic programs) in "seat hours" for accelerated programs often have difficulty explaining why forty hours of classroom instruction, divided into two or three sessions of three hours a week for fifteen weeks is necessarily the ideal. Why not 25-week semesters? Why not three-hour classes? Why not daily classes? The point is that such arrangements have largely been by default, not because of empirical evidence or even theoretical inquiry into best structures for learning.

institutions of higher learning and their practitioners, particularly Christians engaged in the mission of higher education, to navigate through new waters and to emerge both creative and principled.[17]

The first resolution is that *all learning is distance learning.* Alan Hueth addresses this a bit more exuberantly as "oversimplified, reductionist, and limiting notion #1: proximic distance is the only distance to be traversed in education."[18] He is reacting against the common criticism that the "distance" in "distance learning" is a difficult, if not insurmountable obstacle to good learning. Remembering his experiences lecturing to a hall of 150 students, some of whom were engaged in learning, others of whom were not, he noted that

> it eventually became apparent to me that the social nature of education invited all kinds of "distances" to be encountered and traversed. . . . These distances include linguistic, social, psychological, and philosophical differences between individuals (including professors and students) that are created by a variety of intrapersonal and interpersonal factors. Proximic distance is a phenomenon that can affect learning. However, I soon realized that close proximic (face-to-face) distance, alone, did not guarantee that learning would occur. There are other more complex and omnipresent "distances" that are even more real and relevant than proximity that I was also being challenged to traverse. It soon became apparent to me that all learning was "distance learning," with distance being an ever-present, multidimensional, multivariate factor in the learning process that I needed to be aware of and learn more about.[19]

Nontraditional learning environments provide opportunities to traverse some distances that are more difficult to cross in traditional classroom setting. Those whose personality or learning style causes them to shrink back from speaking up in a physical classroom may find it easier to express themselves in an environ-

17. I am particularly indebted here to a single volume of the *Christian Scholar's Review* (33:4 [Summer, 2004]) devoted to the theme of "E-Learning and Christian Higher Education."

18. Hueth, "E-Learning and Christian Higher Education, 529.

19. Ibid.

ment where a posting does not represent an "interruption" of a professor's lecture and where one can choose one's wording carefully rather than risk embarrassment with an impromptu remark. Those who perceive racial or cultural distances in a classroom may find the relative anonymity of the online classroom, where one does not necessarily know the others' racial, ethnic, national, or cultural backgrounds unless that information is voluntarily offered, a safer environment for the learning process. Those who float from classroom to classroom in isolation, confronted each time by a fresh crowd of strangers called "classmates," may find the relational depth and relatively small size of the cohort to be an environment in which one can experience multidirectional learning for the first time. Those who seek regular interactions with instructors who are on campus only three days a week and are available only during specified office hours may find the accessibility of an online instructor by email to be both convenient and conducive to a more productive learning experience. And those who do not have access to traditional higher education because of physical impairment often revel in the freedom to learn (and be in relationship with other learners) in an environment in which their impairments are neutralized or even an advantage.[20]

It is also true that those who wish to use all of the senses simultaneously in the learning process—to hear an instructor speak and to see what she writes on a whiteboard and to touch a specimen passed around the room and to smell the pungency of a colored marker—will find "distance education" a disappointment. Others find comfort in the physical environment of a classroom or discipline in the frequent scheduling of class sessions. For some,

20. "Technology has had a massive impact on the accessibility of information for students with disabilities and has actually removed many barriers to learning. The use of adaptations on personal computers, portable listening and recording devices and so on, allow a student with disabilities to be on an equal footing with their peers. However, if thought is not given to how the technology works for them and whether, for example, a web site is accessible for all students, then this can reverse the process and they can be denied that access which would then lead to social exclusion" (Hope, "Web Accessibility in Higher Education").

distance education is better; for others, it is worse. It all depends on the distance one wishes to traverse.

For Christian institutions, who cannot afford to understand higher education merely as market opportunity, career preparation, citizenship development, or even personal "well-roundedness" (all worthy goals in their own right), but as mission on behalf of the Kingdom of God, distance education is a gift from God. The distance one can traverse through online education, in particular, has implications for the global community of faith. Shirley Roels notes the lack of educational opportunities, particularly for Christians, in many parts of the world. Despite the growth of evangelical institutions worldwide, there are insufficient seats for students, insufficient trained faculty, and insufficient resources to address these problems. The century-old habit of sending the best and brightest from foreign lands to the United States for formal education is not adequate to address the need, nor is it necessarily appropriate to pull a student out of her cultural context for that education. Nor is it financially advisable, given the other options available today.

The other dominant option available today is e-learning. Roels argues,

> Whether we embrace e-learning depends on what we believe to be the mission of Christian higher education institutions that are currently based in Western culture and typically in North America. If the mission is to serve North American youth, then the most that e-learning may provide is an enhancement of their experience, a fringe benefit to the normal residential college experience, or with adult learning, e-learning may provide some access to a second North American population to be served with Christian higher education. However, if the mission of Christian higher education is to disciple the Christians of this world and their cultures, then e-learning provides our best avenue to create global access to deeper Christian learning.[21]

Perhaps that is a distance worth traversing.

Another distance worth traversing is that between private Christian institutions, usually situated in the suburbs of major cities or in small towns in rural states, and the residents of urban

21. Roels, "Global Discipleship and Online Learning," 461.

communities who most need access to self-empowering educational opportunities. Affordable online education, particularly when supplemented by social programs to provide public access to technology, can be accessible to those who would never travel to the suburbs to take high-priced classes through a private Christian college. For Christian universities with an ethos of societal transformation, there are few greater opportunities in the early twenty-first century to live out that ethos, provided that they can overcome the inherent biases against such delivery formats.

A second resolution is that *all learning is mediated by technology*. It is interesting how many professional academics are Luddites at heart, suspicious of or disdainful toward newer technologies that are enhancing their professions. The word "newer" is used quite intentionally here, for many who criticize or reject the technologies of the data video projector or the online course site fail to acknowledge that their preferred forms of teaching are technology-mediated as well. They simply use older technologies.

If a technology is defined as a tool that one utilizes to accomplish a task, then one of the oldest technologies in the educational enterprise is the book.[22] Traditional and nontraditional academics alike read and assign readings in textbooks without necessarily considering the book's advantages and disadvantages as a piece of technology. In fact, it has certain distinct disadvantages compared to more recent technologies. It is certainly not interactive; the book does not respond to questions nor explain itself beyond its initial message. It is difficult to revise or update; revisions require years, not minutes or hours. And even though the technology of creating books is not patented, the production of any single volume requires a considerable financial investment on the part of the author or publisher. It is not a very flexible technology.

Other technologies abound in traditional higher education. The chalkboard (or whiteboard), the flip chart, the overhead pro-

22. "Technology is the set of tools both hardware (physical) and software that help us act and think better. Technology includes all the objects from pencil and paper to the latest electronic gadget" (Stuhlman, "Knowledge Management Terms").

jector and the transparencies upon which the instructor writes, the desk in the front of the room, the rows of chairs with foldable arms for writing, the TV and VCR and the videos that are played on them, the pens and pencil with which students scribble into spiral-bound notebooks, the lecture itself—these are all educational technologies, the utility of which is seldom if ever challenged.

There is room—and need—a deeper discussion about the use of technologies in the learning process, lest we somehow conclude that the choice of any particular technology is a value-neutral or purely methodological decision. David Smith notes that

> If educational technology belonged entirely to the realm of method, and not of meaning, life would be much simpler. If a new technology could be regarded as simply another "routine of efficiency," enhancing learning activities without changing their significance, then the question of whether to adopt it would be a foregone conclusion (as long as there were evidence that the efficiency gains were real). Shifting activities into a medium that made learning more efficient would clearly be a good thing. Of course, the boundaries are not that simple. At a general level, it is widely accepted, almost to the point of cliché, that technological tools are freighted with consequences for our patterns of living.[23]

Smith's caution is appropriate for both newer and older technologies employed in the learning process. As more scholars explore technology and its uses, particularly from a Christian perspective, we will gain fresh understandings of how our assumptions about technological means have impacted our educational ends.[24] We are in need of a theology of technology that takes into account both epistemology and pedagogy.

A final resolution is that *all learning is lifelong*. Gone are the days when there was a clear demarcation between one's years as a student and one's years as a practitioner. Education, even formal education for credits and degrees, is increasingly perceived as a periodic necessity for one's personal and professional development, particularly in a society in which young adults are told to expect to

23. Smith, "Technology and Pedagogical Meaning," 511.

24. Adams, "Technology from a Christian Perspective," 569–79.

change careers five to seven times in their lifetime. Furthermore, we are beginning to appreciate the value of "just-in-time learning,"[25] which is sought and acquired as needed to acquire new skills or perceptions, rather than four or more years of isolation in an artificial environment followed by a lifetime of implementation (or, perhaps more likely, for a career in a field for which one has not been specifically educated).

This provides an opportunity for dialogue between church and academy, as the church has also realized that the process of maturation in the faith, whether termed "Christian education," or "discipleship," or otherwise, is likewise a lifelong endeavor. For two centuries the church borrowed from secular models of education and built classrooms in their worship buildings and outfitted them with chalkboards and desks and bought curriculum from publishing houses and trained teachers to study lesson plans and teach age-specific classes on Sunday mornings in "Sunday School." Christian leaders at the beginning of the twenty-first century are learning that not only were these methods often ineffective in inculcating the disciplines necessary for spiritual nurture and formation, but that they were also failing to do even the one thing they should have done well—to provide a cognitive understanding of the Christian message. The problem of "biblical illiteracy" among those generations raised in Sunday School illustrates this failure all too well.[26]

Michael Polanyi argued in the middle of the twentieth century for a personal or "post-critical" understanding of knowledge (as opposed to an objectivist or Cartesian philosophy).[27] Coming as it did from a member of the scientific community, it startled readers with its rejection of the concept of personal objectivity and neutral knowledge. Those who have followed after have completed the

25. Weinberger, "Just in Time Learning," 623.

26. The charge of biblical illiteracy has been with us for some time and the literature cannot be reviewed here. It is interesting, however, that an Amazon. com search for that phrase results in a book written as early as 1980: Tinknor, *Help Stamp Out Biblical Illiteracy.*

27. Polanyi, *Personal Knowledge.*

revolution by defining knowledge in relational terms, rather than as a "thing" to be acquired or a series of propositions or a collection of data. Christians who have embraced these ideas have done so because of their previous commitment to the notion of relational truth. "I am the way, the truth, and the life," Jesus said, and one need not be a thoroughgoing pietist to apprehend that approaching divine truth meant encountering Christ. To walk with him toward Emmaus and feels our hearts burning within us as he speaks is the desire of the Christian disciple. And that is a lifelong walk.

As both the church and the academy are discovering the need for lifelong learning, there exists now opportunities to cooperate together that had seldom existed before. Instead of sending their teenagers "away" to college, perhaps they can arrange for that formal education can occur within the church community. Instead of sending adults "back" to college, perhaps they can create a culture in which formal education is not a process one leaves on a permanent basis, but is woven into the life of the church. One can glimpse the possibilities of a synergistic relationship in which churches host cohorts of adult learners or provide resources for distance education opportunities and Christian universities provide faculty and curriculum for the training and development of congregational members and church leaders.

This chapter has addressed revolutions in higher education, primarily focused on adult education (although it is hard to imagine why formal education for traditional-aged college students should not eventually follow suit in many respects), and on three resolutions for Christian academics in particular: 1) that all learning is distance learning, 2) that all learning is mediated by technology, and 3) that all learning is lifelong learning. The hope of this author is that these resolutions will provide some level of direction in his own institution and others as they seek to find their way through this revolutionary age.

6

Models of Collaboration

WALKING THE WAY OF COLLABORATION

THIS PROJECT promised one or more models of a collaborative relationship between church and academy in the twenty-first century. The preceding four chapters have delineated the cultural and ideological forces that are causing significant change within both institutions in North America and the forms in which that change is being manifest. This chapter delineates some models by which the church and academy are already poised to enjoy more collaborative relationships—using the three institutions employed as case studies in this book as examples—and as-yet future models that explore two versions of what the future may hold in store. The case studies are supported by personal interviews with the leaders of the three universities.

Surprisingly, the literature of the church/academy relationship supplies few models of its own. Much of the current literature on higher education is fairly critical of the enterprise—of its commercialization or its abandonment of a liberal arts core or its grade inflation or its cooperation with industry or government.[1] One

---

1. See, for instance, Bok, *Universities in the Marketplace*; Hersh and Merrow, *Declining by Degrees*; or Marsden, *The Soul of the American University*.

positive contribution has already been noted: George Keller's telling of the story of Elon University, but this study is the exception that proves the rule.[2] Among Christian universities, the Hughes and Adrian text provides "models" for Christian higher education and Benne compliments six institutions on how they have "kept faith" with their theological traditions, but these are not models of form or function but of expressions of particular confessional groups.[3] And Banks introduces a "missional" model for theological education, but the focus of his discussion is appropriately narrow. This is not to say that the creation of models is not the source of great discussion among academic leaders; it is to argue, however, that studies such as this are necessary in order to create and disseminate models of form and function for the current century.

AN ECUMENICAL MODEL:
HUNTINGTON UNIVERSITY

To say that relations between Huntington University and the Church of the United Brethren in Christ were somewhat strained several years ago is to understate the situation. The university was founded in 1897 as Central College and as the only institution of higher learning of the Church of the United Brethren in Christ (Old Constitution), a relatively small remnant of a fairly nasty schism that had occurred in 1889. Both the college, renamed Huntington in 1917, and the denomination remained relatively small and irrelevant in the larger context of fundamentalist and evangelical Christianity in the twentieth century until fairly recently. The denomination is a longstanding member of the National Association of Evangelicals and has been expanding primarily in other nations or among immigrant communities in the United States in the past 15 years, while losing ground among its traditional base of rural congregations.

2. Keller, *Transforming a College*.

3. Hughes and Adrian, *Models for Christian Higher Education*; Benne, *Quality with Soul*.

The relationship had been deteriorating slightly over the past two decades as the college[4] experienced significant growth in enrollment and the denomination remained relatively stagnant in the United States. A crisis in the relationship occurred in 2002, when a few ministers in the denomination became vocally concerned about the writings of John Sanders, a popular professor of philosophy at the college.[5] Sanders was an advocate both of open theism, a theological innovation that became a source of controversy within the Evangelical Theological Society, and of a version of universalism that at first generated a rather intense level of inquiry. As faculty and staff rallied to Sanders' side, voices in the denomination grew bolder in calling for his immediate ouster. At a meeting of the National Board in April, 2003, the denomination adopted a statement that condemned both open theism and Sanders' understanding of universalism as contrary to the historic teachings of the church and required subscription to such statement by all its ministers.

The college Board of Trustees, heavily populated with United Brethren representatives, opted that Spring to restrict Sanders' teaching to the philosophy classroom and to deny him tenure, choosing instead to grant him a three-year contract that included a buy-out option to be exercised at the discretion of the board. The board utilized that option early in 2005 and Sanders was dismissed at the end of the Spring semester. The National Conference of the Church of the United Brethren, USA, meeting in June, opted to maintain the theological statements adopted two years earlier by the National Board and to keep the following provision in its book of discipline: "When practices, teachings, or decisions within a local church, denominational officials and institutions, or an annual conference challenge the doctrinal integrity (as defined by the Confession of Faith), cooperative relationship, and/or ministry of the Church of the United Brethren in Christ, USA, the US National

---

4. Reflecting a trend among small, private colleges, Huntington College renamed itself Huntington University in July, 2005.

5. See Sanders, *The God Who Risks*.

Conference shall have the authority to apply whatever disciplinary action it considers appropriate."[6]

These actions were not well received on campus (or among Christian academics outside Huntington), where faculty increasingly perceived the denomination as narrow-minded and obsessed with doctrinal trivialities. Many at the college were delighted, therefore, when, in the middle of the controversy, the Executive Leadership Team of the denomination proposed that the U.S. National Conference withdraw from the Church of the United Brethren in Christ, International, and join the Missionary Church, USA. The Missionary Church is an evangelical denomination headquartered in nearly Fort Wayne, Indiana, that has experienced considerable growth in churches and membership in the past two decades. Disbanding the denomination would have provided the college with an opportunity to become independent of any denominational control, as the Missionary Church owned Bethel College in nearby Mishawaka, Indiana, and would have been unlikely to support two very similar institutions of higher education within the same region of Indiana.

The proposal to disband the denomination failed in the Fall of 2004, in part due to efforts by a grassroots group called UBHope, which was advocating for a restart of the United Brethren movement in a manner consonant with its founding principles and in forms appropriate for a twenty-first century postmodern cultural context.[7] The United Brethren membership failed to ratify the proposal and the quadrennial National Conference, which met in June, 2005, was forced to consider other options. This meant, of course, that there has existed an opportunity to reframe the relationship between the denomination and its sole institution of higher learning. President G. Blair Dowden, who has led Huntington since

6. *Discipline of the Church of the United Brethren in Christ USA*, 605.10.

7. I played a leading role in the UBHope movement and was particularly involved in occasional public articulations of its intentions and aims. The primary articulation, entitled "The Original Spirit in Twenty-First Century Clothes," was presented to the U.S. National Board at Huntington College, Huntington, Indiana, 14 February 2005.

1991, has noted that there has been a weakening of the relationship in recent years and that the university would pursue a more non-denominational or inter-denominational identity in the coming years.[8]

Drawing on the formulations of George Keller of Roanoke College,[9] however, Dowden suggested factors at play that could yet strengthen or weaken the relationship. The first is the employment of faculty from the sponsoring denomination. On the one hand, this is a problem for there are precious few from which to draw; this author is one of only two or three United Brethren scholars not already serving on the faculty or in the administration of Huntington University. There were more United Brethren faculty members thirty years ago. On the other hand, many—at least half, he notes—new faculty members at Huntington become members of nearby United Brethren churches. Further, several Huntington University faculty members have played leading roles (e.g. the National Board or Executive Leadership Team) in the national church.[10] There is no doubt that the kind of faculty members recruited by an institution will have a greater effect on its long-term character than any particular administration, given the longevity and freedom that tenure bestows.

Another factor affecting the relationship is the number of students provided to the institution by the sponsoring denomination. While never high, this number has declined in both actual numbers and in the percentage of the total student body in the last decade. The university's preference for a single-campus, residential model of higher education has also limited its accessibility to non-traditional United Brethren students, most of whom reside too far from Huntington to participate in its largely residential program offerings. And its trend toward self-identification as a broadly

8. Interviewed 18 July 2005 by phone.

9. See Keller, *Transforming a College* and *Academic Strategy*.

10. Dowden personally interviews all faculty candidates at Huntington. This reflects both the relative size of the institution (about one-third the student body of George Fox or Eastern) and his own commitment to maintain the spiritual and academic vitality of the institution.

evangelical institution has, paradoxically, limited its appeal to those who would be attracted to a uniquely United Brethren educational context. Why go to Huntington if it is identical in mission and culture to a CCCU institution closer home?

Financial support is yet another factor in the relationship between a college and its sponsoring church. Dowden noted that the support given through the denominational budget has been reduced dramatically in the past 20 years. This decrease probably represents two influences. The first is a perception within the church that the college, which has resources far beyond that of the denomination, is financially self-sufficient and does not really need the paltry sums included in its budget for institutional support. The second is an intentional trend, beginning in 1993, to downsize the national budget for the denomination by decreasing personnel and by funneling support for missions and education through local churches, rather than collecting and distributing it on the local level. It is likely, however, that local church financial support for the university has probably declined along with the decrease in funds from the national budget.

How, then, can Huntington University nurture a more collaborative relationship with the Church of the United Brethren in Christ in the generation to come? And how can other institutions of higher education, with similar struggles with their sponsoring denominations, do likewise? The answer may come from the fourth and final factor discussed by Dowden—a shared theology. Dowden notes that "we have some of that" but that there was greater theological overlap thirty years ago. The university is strongly evangelical, he observes, "maybe more so than the United Brethren Church." What he apparently means by this is not merely adherence to the theological tenets of American evangelicalism, but the application of these tenets in evangelism, service, and mission. This, intentionally or not, is a gently worded indictment of the United Brethren Church of the early twenty-first century, for it was born out of the revivals of the Great Awakening and came into its own during the social reform and missionary movements of the early to mid-nineteenth century. It is—or at least has been—"evangelical" in every connotation of that word. If it were to be no longer generally perceived as such, it must recover some of its original spirit.

Yet it has also been strangely ecumenical. The United Brethren movement was founded by German revivalists of the Mennonite, Reformed, and Lutheran traditions who were bound by a common experience and message (the necessity of conversion), not by institutional identity. One founder, Philip Wilhelm Otterbein, never fully abandoned his relationship with the German Reformed Classis that had ordained him and the other, Martin Boehm, although excommunicated from the Mennonite Church due to his close association with those who justified war, among other reasons, joined a Methodist class meeting before his death. Both were serving simultaneously as bishops of the Church of the United Brethren in Christ.

Because of different traditions that came together in its founding, it has become part of the heritage of the United Brethren to remain broadly ecumenical within the evangelical tradition. (This is what made the 2003 doctrinal statement against open theism and universalism such an anomaly and—to this author, a disappointment—in the United Brethren story.) The United Brethren have consistently refused to declare an eschatological position, for instance, preferring instead to insist on the imminent return of Christ and leaving the field open for differing opinions. Likewise, they take no stand on baptism (except that it ought to be practiced) and thereby respected both the Anabaptist and Reformed elements in their heritage. They have a bold but brief Confession of Faith that is attractive to those from other, more narrowly-defined traditions who are considering a relationship with the United Brethren. A healthy percentage[11] of its ministers are imports from other evangelical or even non-evangelical denominations, drawn by its broadminded evangelicalism. As Superintendent of Church Multiplication and Urban Ministries for the MidAtlantic

11. As far as I can determine, the exact number has never been calculated.

Conference of the denomination for nine years, I had the opportunity to assist in the establishment of eighteen new United Brethren congregations (from a starting point of 42) and to welcome a considerable number of non-UB ministers and even a few non-UB congregations into full fellowship, largely because of this heritage.

This dual evangelical-ecumenical identity is something now shared (at least in theory) by both the denomination and the university. If Huntington University is intent on building on its reputation as a regionally-ranked, solidly-evangelical institution with a vibrant spiritual life and a service ethos, then perhaps it can do so in partnership with a denomination that is once again claiming its heritage as a movement with a vibrant spirituality, a social reform ethos, and an ecumenical heart. In short, while they have been changing independently of each other, both institutions are now in a position where they are claiming identities that are remarkably similar in scope and spirit. This is an opportunity to be exploited.

What could a relationship built upon these similarities look like in practice? First, both institutions should continue to intentionally recruit and attract highly-qualified personnel (particularly faculty and clergy) from the wider evangelical community. Both church and academy are attractive to others for the same reasons. Second, both institutions should return the favor by using their resources to support the "church at large" rather than purely parochial concerns. The university currently does this better than the church, but the denomination must learn to adopt what some in positions of leadership call a "kingdom mindset." Both the proposal to disband and join the Missionary Church and the UBHope proposal were predicated on this ecumenical commitment. Third, the Education Commission of the denomination, which currently concerns itself solely with the affairs of the university, must broaden its scope to address the creation of a more literate culture within the United Brethren community, which will mean occasionally directing United Brethren students into other institutions of higher education, as Huntington is unable to meet all of the higher education needs of a national church. Fourth, the United Brethren leadership must recognize that Huntington University has quite outgrown the denomination—that the relationship henceforth must be one of unequal partners, not of ownership and control.

These changes will be more difficult for the church than for the academy, for it would require the United Brethren to begin understanding themselves as a post-denominational denomination—one that exists not for its distinctives but for its peculiar and powerful commonness. If this is achieved, however, it may be that within a decade or so, identification with the United Brethren Church will be considered by the university as neither an irrelevancy nor a handicap, but a recognizable and logical expression of the institution's own identity and mission.

Other institutions and denominations may also profit from this model. One of the primary reasons for tension between church and academy in the twentieth century is the desire of the institutions of higher education to broaden their appeal beyond what is often perceived as a more narrow focus of the sponsoring denomination. But, as noted earlier in this volume, denominationalism itself is undergoing an examination that will eventually require that existing judicatories either broaden their self-definitions, beyond increasingly irrelevant distinctions of picayune theological positions, or face marginalization in a society that is no longer interested in many such matters, rooted as they are in the rationalism of the modernist era. As denominations increasingly see opportunities for partnerships with others who share common values and beliefs, they may find themselves sharing an outlook toward their "market" that may differ less from that of their institutions of higher learning than was true a decade ago. And perhaps those institutions may return the favor by honoring those distinctions that continue to matter in the era that is emerging.

AN INCARNATIONAL MODEL:
EASTERN UNIVERSITY

Eastern University is an unusual school in several respects. While it advertises itself as "theologically conservative," its faculty represents a far wider spectrum of Christianity than is found at most CCCU institutions and articulate a wider range of theological positions. It has a reputation for being theologically "liberal" in some conservative circles. Ironically, the individual who, more than anyone, supported a conservative, orthodox theological position in public debates with John Sanders of Huntington was Christopher Hall, then professor of theology and now chancellor of Eastern.[12] It also has a reputation for being politically liberal, and this reputation is well-deserved. For example, Eastern's best-known spokesperson, Tony Campolo, was publicly identified with Bill Clinton during the Monica Lewinksy scandal and has been an advocate for left-wing political causes for most of his career. Much of this political liberalism stems from a very strong commitment to social justice; in fact, President David Black's recurring theme for his administration is "the integration of faith, reason, and justice."

Eastern expresses this combination of a broadly ecumenical understanding of its faith (which is, it should be noted, accompanied by a rather vibrant and quite explicit spirituality) and a commitment to social transformation through a variety of unique programs: one of its campuses is located in urban Philadelphia and through it students can both study and apply what they learn in their urban studies programs; the School of Leadership and Development offers graduate programs in economic development and organizational leadership a number of locations worldwide; the Nueva Esperanza Center for Higher Education (NECHE) operates a junior college for the Hispanic community in north Philadelphia as a branch campus of Eastern; the People for People Institute provides undergraduate programs for the working poor in urban Philadelphia; and, finally, Palmer Theological Seminary, located right on the city line, operates degree and non-degree programs for urban ministers at various locations throughout

12. See, for instance, their debates in back-to-back issues of *Christianity Today.* Sanders and Hall, "Does God Know Your Next Move?"

southeastern Pennsylvania, as well as a rural West Virginia extension program.[13]

The word that best expresses the commitment behind these
and other efforts is "incarnation." Rather than merely expecting
students to leave home and live in the rather tony Philadelphia
suburb of St. Davids for four years, Eastern University locates itself
where its students live and serve and does so with such agility that
there is probably no single person in the university who can identify all of the class sites in use at any given time. This observation
does not even take into account those students who are enrolled at
Eastern through programs that are entirely or primarily online.

Incarnational presence is what Frost and Hirsch have called
the church to practice as well—to go beyond an "attractional"
model that seeks to draw large numbers of people to a central location and to pursue an incarnational model that moves outward
into the communities where people live.[14] It might be expressed
as the difference between the marketing and growth strategies of
Wal-Mart and Starbucks. Wal-Mart builds huge "supercenters," at
which they display and sell nearly everything one once looked for
in a shopping mall and surround them with massive parking lots
to accommodate the throngs that drive to shop at their stores.[15]
Starbucks, on the other hand, multiplies itself through the planting
of small shops in thousands of locations around the world, some
just blocks from others. They seek out where their customers live
and work and start a coffee shop within that mileau; as a result,
many of their customers walk to the store, rather than drive.[16]

In ministry terms, the megachurch follows the Wal-Mart
model and the house or cell church the Starbucks model. Similarly,
in academic terms, the huge state universities have adopted the

13. Eastern boasts of approximately 4000 total students.

14. Frost and Hirsch, *The Shaping of Things to Come.*

15. In fairness, it should be noted that Wal-Mart's aggressive growth in
small cities and rural areas, long ignored by previous retail chains, should
certainly be considered incarnational as well.

16. Schultz, *Pour Your Heart Into It;* and Slater, *The Wal-Mart Decade.*

Wal-Mart vision and a growing number of schools are exploring the Starbucks vision. Some of these schools are traditional schools reinventing themselves, like Eastern, and others are young upstarts, like the University of Phoenix, which hosts nearly a half a million students without a home campus.[17]

Incarnational strategies provide opportunities for Eastern and schools like it to form more collaborative relationships with the Church, as courses can be delivered to nearly any site that is accessible to students and faculty, including church buildings. Congregations that are beginning to discover that their Christian education programs are failing to address the higher-level intellectual, vocational, and spiritual formation needs of their parishioners may choose to partner with a Christian university to host a course or series of courses, a certificate program, a degree program, or an ongoing lifelong learning venture. Indeed, Eastern has experimented with these ideas but primarily in partnership with the parachurch (e.g. World Vision, Young Life, Habitat with Humanity) and, increasingly, with congregational or denominational expressions of the People of God. Needless to say, this kind of approach would also provide the opportunity to reconnect with the American Baptist denomination, whose relationship with Eastern is today largely a matter of heritage and mutual respect, rather than any significant collaboration.

An incarnational strategy could also have the reverse effect of inviting or encouraging congregations to become more active on the campuses of the university. Christian colleges and universities have historically drawn students out of local churches into an intense (yet in some ways artificial) Christian community on campus, complete with cell groups, ministry opportunities, large worship gatherings (chapel), Christian education, and even "youth group" activities. Very few congregations can rival the energy, relational depth, or emotional intensity of such communities and it is thus one of the ironies of Christian colleges that many of their

17. University of Phoenix, "Just the Facts." http://www.phoenix.edu/about _us/media_relations/just-the-facts.html.

Christian students do not actively participate in the life of a congregation, sometimes even after graduation. Should local congregations choose to establish a physical presence on campus (beyond the activities of denominational student ministries), however, they may be able to engage students in the real life of a multigenerational Christian community—and even keep a number of those students involved in the life of that congregation following graduation. Christian college campuses may be great places to start some very interesting church plants as well.

Eastern's "unusual" nature is right now its greatest strength, for it is only slightly ahead of the curve in terms of future trends in higher education. Other enterprising institutions are taking advantage of this incarnational model. One can only hope, for the sake of the Kingdom of God, that there will be many such enterprising institutions in the years to come. One can imagine a future in which students do not "go away" to college but college comes to them, a future in which it will be increasingly difficult to answer the questions, "Where is your school located?" and "Where is your church located?" That preferred future will have embraced an incarnational philosophy that emphasizes presence over place.

A CONTEXTUAL MODEL: GEORGE FOX UNIVERSITY

In 1996, George Fox College bought and took over operations of Western Evangelical Seminary in nearby Portland, Oregon, and renamed itself George Fox University; the seminary was renamed George Fox Evangelical Seminary in 2000. The university had previously begun a professional studies program and had expanded its locations to include Eugene, Oregon, and Boise, Idaho, in addition to the campus in Newberg and the seminary location in Portland. Through acquisition, program development, and site expansion, George Fox's enrollment has more than quadrupled in size over the past two decades to reach its current enrollment of over 3300 total students.[18] The university has demonstrated an ability to be

18. George Fox University, "Quick Facts." http://www.georgefox.edu/about/quick_facts/index.html.

fairly agile[19] in its marketplace, particularly considering that it is located in Oregon, which is increasingly secular in orientation, and that both Western Seminary and Multnomah Bible College and Biblical Seminary, also located in Portland, represent "competitors" quite close to home.

It is on George Fox Evangelical Seminary that this discussion is focused, however. It has been argued that most seminaries and schools of theological education in the United States (and elsewhere) follow models that do not best serve either their students or the congregations those students serve. Robert Banks, for instance, observes that

> Many pastors and denominational leaders have asked whether seminaries provide their graduates with the kind of knowledge and expertise that they need to fulfill their ministry responsibilities. There is much talk about the widening gap between the seminary and the church, part of it stemming from the fact that these days less faculty have ministry experience. Concern about this leads to various educational innovations and in-service programs or, on occasion, to struggles for political control between denominational authorities and seminary boards. Similar criticism has come more recently from postdenominational megachurches and house churches. Both of these criticize the way theological institutions take people away from their local setting and fail to give them the practical habits and skills they require for effective ministry.[20]

Banks, however, does note that the number of full-time students at most seminary campuses has been falling (this trend has continued since the publication of his volume in 1999) due to changing student profiles. More older students enter seminary already engaged in full-time ministry or as a step toward a second career; the number of part-time students is growing. Rather than

19. The word "agile" in this section is derived from Peter Senge's description of "the learning organization" as one that is capable of fairly quick changes in structure, service, or product without concomitant adjustments of mission or vision. Senge, *The Fifth Discipline*.

20. Banks, *Re-envisioning Theological Education*, 11. See also Oden, *Requiem*.

being a purely negative trend, however, this has presented the opportunity, however, to engage students in just-in-time learning as more are able to practice what they are learning, rather than storing up ideas and principles for some future use.

George Fox Evangelical Seminary, through the creative leadership of its two most recent deans, Jules Glanzer (now president of Tabor College in Kansas) and Chuck Conniry, has capitalized on these trends, not by abandoning the notion of traditional, residential seminary education but by creating alternate options for those already engaged in ministry. Furthermore, those options are generally perceived as "cutting-edge," addressing timely issues and trends that most other evangelical seminaries are only now beginning to recognize (and criticize). This desire to be contextual, even trendy, is reflected well in the published "distinctives" of the seminary, which include the following statements:

> Culturally relevant: The society in which our students serve is culturally diverse, postmodern, and postdenominational. The faculty understands this context and prepares students for effective ministry in a diverse world. Students are encouraged to confront and address the pressing issues of our world and to meet societal and personal needs in a responsively creative and culturally relevant way . . .
>
> Technologically integrated: The seminary uses information technology to provide students with the best theological education possible and to help students prepare more effective strategies for ministry. Many courses are Web-enhanced and some are offered online. "Smart classrooms" provide a learning experience that models creative ministry through the use of technology.[21]

Nowhere are these commitments seen more clearly than in the Doctor of Ministry program of which I am an alumnus. While many other schools are adopting an oppositional stance toward the postmodern culture, George Fox is assisting students in learning to speak its language and minister in that context. While many other schools are requiring students to travel to campus, George

21. George Fox Evangelical Seminary, "Distinctives." http://www.george-fox.edu/seminary/about/distinctives.html.

Fox is offering Doctor of Ministry through an innovative delivery system that combines online collaboration, occasional residencies, and attendance at seminars chosen by the student. While many other schools are relying primarily or solely on long-time faculty members who are not always conversant with current issues in ministry, George Fox contracts with very well-known and well-respected experts from across the nation to serve as instructors and mentors in the program. This student was delighted at the opportunity to learn under the tutelage of Leonard Sweet, for instance, an opportunity that would not have been available to him were it not for the nontraditional delivery of this program. This reflects not only strong recruiting on the part of the director and dean, but also a willingness to utilize short-term faculty to lead adaptable programs.[22]

This approach has been very intentional on the part of the seminary. Glanzer's original vision for theological education encompassed a new model of church/academy partnership, which instituted and integrated at George Fox:

> The current model is to call out the gifted and godly, send them to school, and then have them serve in another context than the one from which they were called. The new model will allow for the called ones to remain where they are and serve while at the same time receive the needed education. Training will be contextualized and done in partnership with the church. No longer will seminaries say, "Send us your students and we will train them and then they can go to another church to serve." Rather we will partner together in the training and the calling group will experience the fruits of the training.[23]

These innovations, of course, have been of greater value to the Church at large than to the four denominations that sponsor the university: the Evangelical Friends, Free Methodist Church, Wesleyan Church, and Evangelical Church of North America.

22. Other well-known scholars and practitioners recruited at various times for the Doctor of Ministry tracks include Brennan Manning, Dallas Willard, Tony Campolo, and Sam Rima.

23. Interviewed 4 August 2005, email.

Three additional groups provide students but no financial support: Presbyterian Church of America, Evangelical Covenant Church, and Foursquare Gospel. Glanzer noted that George Fox under his leadership saw itself as "a post-denominational seminary. . . . I do not see a strong relationship [in the future] between denominations and seminaries."[24] His approach was to address the church at large while also "customizing" the seminary's relationship with each of these sponsoring or supporting groups in order to maintain or further those relationships.

Former President H. David Brandt, under whose leadership the Seminary was acquired and the college transitioned to a University with a wider appeal to the evangelical community, noted that "the relationship with the Northwest Yearly Meeting of Friends, which is the university's chief denominational constituency, is very strong and very cordial." However, "at this time the university has a far larger budget and constituency than the Yearly Meeting" (a situation analogous to that of Huntington University and the United Brethren) and thus Brandt predicts that "the church will continue to be an important voice in the operation of the university, but that control will become less direct than it is now." This seems to be the case under the recent leadership of his successor, Robin Baker.

Brandt, who had previously served Tabor and Messiah Colleges in high-level administrative roles, articulated an approach to collaboration that appears to be more relational and attitudinal than institutional: "I sometimes summarize my opinions about church/university relationships by suggesting that the church has been too critical of the university, but that the university has been too arrogant toward the church. I then suggest that both church and university could unilaterally decide to be less critical or arrogant. My suggestion has been to the university that we choose to be less arrogant. It might be interesting to see what could happen if our attitudes were to change."[25]

24. Ibid.
25. Interviewed 11 July 2005, email.

Glanzer's words were almost identical: "In my opinion, the academy needs to shed some of its arrogance, and the church needs to not be so critical." For the relationship between church and academy in the twenty-first century, this approach may well be the wisest and most effective of all. One of the most telling critiques of mega–churches (and others) about seminaries is that they are not terribly relevant to the needs of those in current ministry. The extent to which that critique has merit differs from institution to institution . . . and by what one expects of graduate theological education. Nevertheless, this critique illustrates the necessity of listening: the academy listening to the church about what it aspires to be, what it needs of its leaders, what its challenges are in a new generation. This will involve, for a time at least, resisting the temptation to "tell": to tell the church what it needs, what it should be thinking, how it should be acting. That ministry, too, is needed . . . but only the church has been honored and respected enough to be heard. And those institutions that hear well will prosper.

A VIRTUAL MODEL: UNIVERSITY 21

The three preceding vignettes were drawn from existing strengths in existing universities; they reveal that more collaborative relationships between church and academy are already possible in the current environment. All three of these institutions were just a few years ago quite small (student enrollment in the hundreds, not thousands), residential liberal arts colleges that appealed primary to traditional-aged undergraduates from the sponsoring denomination or others similar to it. All three—and others like them— have remade themselves in light of twenty-first century cultural realities and are prospering as a result. And all three have available to them the ecumenical, incarnational, and contextual models for creative collaboration.

What if one had a different starting-point, however? What if one could build a brand new Christian university during this first quarter of the twenty-first century and do so without imposing on it the assumptions and structures of the past? What if one could create a new learning environment that would serve to strengthen the Church while meeting the educational needs of a diverse and widespread student body? How would such a university look? The question is relevant because one cannot assume that the current institutions will remain the only players in the coming century, and because the new for-profit universities are changing the rules rather dramatically. It is time for Christian academicians to think through basic assumptions. Therefore, the following three principles constitute some preliminary speculation in answer to those questions.

First, the hypothetical university (labeled "University 21" for our purposes here) will exist wherever a community or learners gathers, be that on a university campus, in a corporate board room, in a church classroom, in a private family room, in the back room of a restaurant, or online (perhaps in a third world nation). Perhaps the single greatest technological and cultural transformation to impact higher education in the twenty-first century is its liberation from the constraints of geography. University 21 will be simultaneously global and local ("glocal"). Most universities have not yet discovered the potential of this seeming paradox, but a host of new, largely for-profit institutions have. The University of Phoenix, Capella University, Nova Southeastern, and others of their ilk are drawing students by the thousands because of their ability to transcend campus boundaries. One dare not call these secular, for-profit ventures "incarnational," at least not in the theological sense of the word, and their critics are too often correct in noting deficiencies in both the quality of the academic offerings and the student services.

Yet these institutions do represent at least one version of the future of higher education; it is time that a Christian institution with a stronger ethos, a more powerful mission, and higher academic standards illustrates how a boundaryless university can actually function to the betterment of its students, the Church, and the world. Grand Canyon University, a for-profit Christian

institution in Arizona, is attempting this model (see www.gcu.
edu); others, perhaps without the profit motive, will likely do so in
the coming decade. Interestingly, in light of the shrinking global
economy, the creation of a boundaryless university requires less
capital than the founding of a traditional school, and the availabil-
ity (or lack thereof) of capital is one of the primary limiting factors of Christian institutions of higher learning in North America
and elsewhere.

Second, University 21 will recognize that while there is always a vocational demand for degree programs, adult students in
particular are increasingly seek flexible learning experiences more
than merely academic degrees. Therefore, it will offer a variety of
academic experiences, including for-credit and not-for-credit options, individual courses, packages of courses that may or may not
result in the awarding of a certificate, degree programs (including
innovative interdisciplinary degrees), seminars, and book studies.
The days in which "college" was primary about providing a baccalaureate degree to a 22-year-old and a master's degree to an elite few
who soldiered on past that age are over; the twenty-first century is
an era of lifelong learning. If the universities do not provide those
learning experiences, their students will go elsewhere—to motiva-
tional seminars at the local Holiday Inn, to the books and videos
of the latest pop-culture guru (even or especially among evangelicals), to the online and twenty-four-hour media news sources. And
they will be right to do so, even if the product they buy in those
venues leaves much to be desired. For institutions of higher education seeking students, there is a market that is still largely untapped
because of prevailing assumptions about the forms that higher
education must take. University 21 will operate without those
assumptions and will reach that market. And, if its mission as a
Christian institution means anything, it will transform that market.
A "market," after all, is merely a collection of people—redeemed or
redeemable—with shared characteristics.

A third principle on which University 21 will operate is that
of sharing of intellectual capital. One form in which this will take

place is open source curriculum. This concept rejects the curricular forms dominant in Western higher education and their proprietary implications and substitutes a form drawn from open source software (e.g., the Linux operating system). Proprietary software contains a source code that is owned by someone—usually the company selling the product. The buyer or end user may use the software but may not adapt it for one's own use or legally distribute it to others. Open source software, on the other hand, is "owned" by the community of users; its source code is open and rewritable. Those who make adaptations to the software may freely share such adaptation with others, who may make their own. Similarly, most forms of curricular design—syllabi, textbooks, etc.—are proprietary in nature. They are owned by the faculty member, the institution, or the publisher. While it is likely impossible that publishers will opt for open source texts, University 21 can choose to deny itself and its faculty proprietary rights on its syllabi and lesson plans. They will belong to the community of users, faculty and students alike, as well as to those outside of the university who discover them and adapt them for their own use.

This is not as far-fetched or unrealistic as it may sound. While the dominance of Blackboard™ among online learning platforms has made online education even more proprietary than in the past, other models are beginning to be explored, including the free, open-source platform known as Moodle. Furthermore, there has been a flurry of growth in online academic journals (of varying quality), many of which are available to the general public at no charge, and an online directory that collects data on them (www .doaj.org). The question for University 21 is whether it wishes to regard its intellectual capital as solely a revenue-creating opportunity or whether there is opportunity to share ideas in a free and open academic marketplace in addition to the necessary collection of tuition and other forms of revenue. Can the profit motive be put aside, at least in part, in order to better fulfill the mission of Christian higher education?

The question of intellectual capital and revenue sharing concerns faculty most of all. University 21 will have a faculty and it will hopefully be an esteemed collection of scholars, teachers, and practitioners. But its faculty will differ in some important aspects from those of traditional universities. For one thing, the status distinctions between full-time and part-time faculty members will be largely abolished; promotions and rewards will be based upon factors such as performance, contribution, and commitment, and not solely on the extent or duration of one's contract. Some faculty members will be engaged only occasionally, when a community of learners has been gathered who wish to learn what one has to offer or when available due to other (perhaps full-time) commitments, including contracts at other institutions. Some will teach or write year-round. Some will primarily pursue a research agenda and thus contribute to the university (and the world) by distributing their research in media that are highly accessible to those who need to know (i.e., both scholarly and non-scholarly sources). Some will specialize in the art of teaching and direct most of their energies there. Others will serve effectively as academic administrators, ensuring quality and appropriateness of the ever-changing curriculum. Faculty members will be encouraged to become co-learners in disciplines outside of their specialties, thus contributing to the creation of a community of learners where traditional distinctions between students and faculty will occasionally become blurred.

These three principles—geographical transcendence, flexible learning packages, and the sharing of intellectual capital—constitute the core of a new vision for a Christian university. How, then, do these principles contribute to a greater collaboration between church and academy? For one thing, University 21 will be able to easily become incarnate within any local congregation that can muster enough students to create a cohort of learners (or any congregation may recommend University 21 to individual members due to its accessibility and flexibility). Furthermore, it will support the work of traditional Christian universities (at least those that are adaptable enough to partner with it) while seeking to meet needs that are not addressed by the more geographically-restricted institutions. It will easily create courses or programs or seminars to address the needs of a denomination or congregation or para-church organization and will provide that sponsoring organization with the curriculum to adapt it and distribute it as needed for their own purposes. It will sponsor needed research by Christian scholars and make that research accessible to the Christian community. Finally, and perhaps most significantly, it will allow fellow Christians in other parts of the world to have access to a high-quality Christian learning experience and to adapt that learning for their own cultural context.

One of the primary questions regarding this model is its practicality (particularly in financial terms) in an era in which economic pressures are requiring institutions to take fewer risks and to make the most benefit from every dollar. Table 1, below, presents some preliminary thoughts regarding a business model for University 21, as compared to a "traditional university." Defining a traditional university is difficult for, as the case studies in this book reveal, even the Christian universities that are members of the Council of Christian Colleges and Universities are very different. The descriptions, therefore, are intended to be very, very general. Describing University 21 is even more difficult, both for the fact that it does not yet exist and for the realization that, by definition, the institutions that adopt this model will vary far more widely than traditional schools have. Nevertheless, the model does lead to certain conclusions regarding key components of any institution of higher education and they are thus noted here. The components are followed by summary statements in which it is noted that the University 21 model should be at least as financially solvent as the traditional model.

TABLE 1. FINANCIAL MODEL OF UNIVERSITY 21

	Traditional University	University 21
Physical Facilities	The traditional university has an extensive investment in one or more physical campuses; these properties, which are increasingly luxurious and modern, are typically worth hundreds of millions of dollars. They represent a tremendous investment of capital resources and their maintenance and use represents a substantial portion of the university's annual operating budget. Furthermore, the cost of installing and maintaining an appropriate technology infrastructure has grown substantially, both in terms of expectations and of budgets.	Because University 21 will be large a "virtual" university, it will rely primarily on facilities provided by others in order to offer its services. This approach has its drawbacks; the opportunity to offer a central athletic program, for instance, would be minimal. However, this would permit capital funds that would otherwise be invested in facilities to be utilized otherwise. Operating costs on facilities, however, may be greater, as they would likely include leases for classroom and office facilities in multiple locations. It is assumed that most classes taught onsite in churches (or at the facilities of other partners) would require minimal expenditures. Technology expenses will be substantial; however, the infrastructure will be more virtual than physical for University 21.
Student Population	The traditional university seeks to convert part-time students into full-time students, as many infrastructure and service costs are uniform, irrespective of the numbers of credits sought by the student. Total student enrollment is usually measured in FTEs (full-time enrollment) and perhaps	Because University 21 will be built upon a lifelong learner model, it assumes that the average student will enroll for a course, a certificate, a major or minor, and then return at a later date for additional coursework. The result will be an FTE that is rather low (perhaps as low as 50%) but a student population that at any

	Traditional University	University 21
Student Population (cont.)	three-quarters of the total student body is comprised of full-time students in defined degree programs.	given moment could reach the tens of thousands (something no explicitly Christian university in the U.S. has yet achieved). In fact, total enrollment will become very difficult to track, as it will fluctuate widely from one week to the next, as traditional semester models of learning (designed for residential students) are supplemented by just-in-time and flexible deliveries.
Faculty	The traditional university has found itself using part-time adjunct faculty more often in recent decades, yet there remains a basic commitment among most Christian institutions (which are primarily identified as teaching—as opposed to research—institutions) that most (usually 75% or more) classes will be taught by full-time faculty. The personnel costs associated with this commitment represent the single largest portion of the instructional budget of a school.	Because University 21 will utilize a decentralized model of instructional delivery, the gathering of a substantial full-time faculty into a single location would be counterproductive. There will be full-time faculty members; however, they will be utilized in a broader range of services than their traditional counterparts. Some will be program directors, assuming responsibility for the academic quality of the curriculum and instruction in a particular academic program.Some will be instructional designers and content experts, utilizing their knowledge and skills to create quality curriculum for use across the university. Some will be full-time researchers (a luxury few Christian institutions can currently afford).

	Traditional University	University 21
Faculty (cont.)		And while some will be full-time teachers, most instructors will be contracted to teach individual courses. The ratio of full-time to part-time (or contracted) faculty will likely be approximately 1 to 4. On the other hand, it is time that Christian institutions follow the lead of larger, secular universities and begin providing equitable compensation and benefits for part-time faculty, as well as input into the governance of the institution.
Fundraising & Development	The traditional university is heavily dependent upon fundraising efforts by its president, development team, deans, and (increasingly) faculty in order to sustain operations and expand facilities, an important factor in a very competitive market. Periodic funding campaigns now range into the tens of millions of dollars and endowments are reaching those levels. Such high endowments are necessary in order to offset the real cost of tuition, particularly for residential students.	Because University 21 will not invest heavily in the kinds of things that attract large gifts (such as buildings), it could be deprived of some significant funding sources. This loss, however, would be offset by its ability to attract adult students with its lifelong learning models. Because of employer-sponsored tuition reimbursement, generous government-sponsored student loan programs, and their ability to earn a living while studying, adult students are often able to pay tuition rates that are not dependent on endowment-supported discounts. And adult alumni are able to contribute more quickly and at higher rates than 22-year-old alumni.

	Traditional University	University 21
Fundraising & Develop- ment (cont.)		They are also able to assist their alma mater in securing additional partnerships for specialized offerings (e.g. a Human Resources certificate for employees in their company).
Summary	The traditional university invests heavily in physical facilities and instructional personnel. Funding is derived primarily from endowment-supported tuition income and capital gifting.	University 21 invests less in physical facilities and instructional personnel, but more in technology and operations. It profits less from gifts but derives greater tuition revenue, which is substantially higher due to increased student enrollment.

There are, of course, many questions that yet need to be answered and it is perhaps useful to point out once again here that these are mere speculations of the most abstract sort. What will be the quality of its academic offerings if they are in nearly constant revision by the end user and if large numbers of the faculty are operating largely on the periphery? Would it truly support the work of traditional Christian universities or would it cut into their markets? Would it become just a Christian version of the University of Phoenix? Is this model too counter-cultural to be successful? Or, to the contrary, is this model too trendy, too ephemeral to have any longstanding academic or ministry value? They are good questions, and the answers await those who experiment, risk, create, and evaluate in the years ahead.

A MERGER MODEL:
INDIANA CHRISTIAN UNIVERSITY

What, then, do existing colleges do? This study has already explored and articulated how three particular universities can build upon existing strengths and position themselves well in this emergent culture. Others can do similar things. But perhaps there are even more radical options available to these institutions. Indeed, as Christian schools move aggressively toward the creation of off-campus classrooms and multi-campus models at the same time that they are eschewing narrow denominational identities in favor of more inclusive ones, they will increasingly be forced to justify their separate existences. For instance, in the late nineteenth and early twentieth centuries, it may have made sense for Christians in Indiana to establish a college in Goshen (Goshen College) and another in Mishawaka (Bethel College) and a third in Huntington (Huntington University) and a fourth in Upland (Taylor University) and a fifth in Marion (Indiana Wesleyan University) and a sixth in Anderson (Anderson University), and a seventh in Winona Lake (Grace College). All seven of these institutions are members of the CCCU and all, with the possible exception of Goshen, which maintains a strong institutional and public commitment to the Mennonite Church, are seeking to broaden their appeal beyond a narrow denominational focus. They are becoming, in other words, somewhat redundant.

A commitment to good stewardship of the resources of the Kingdom will eventually call upon these schools (and others) to relationships of collaboration, sharing programs, faculty, libraries, and campuses, and granting students easy access to and transferability of credits and program offerings of the other schools. One version of that sharing would be the creation of what is here called "Indiana Christian University" (ICU) through a merger of these seven institutions. As demonstrated by Table 2 (below), the combined institution would enroll approximately 26,000 students, putting it in the ranks of major state universities and providing it opportunities not available to schools of 1000-2000 residential students. (It should be noted that the majority of these students are drawn from a single school—Indiana Wesleyan—due largely to the more than 12,500 students in its expansive adult and professional studies programs.)

TABLE 2. COMPARISON OF INDIANA INSTITUTIONS

Institution	Enrollment*	Affiliation	Location	Website
Anderson University	2750	Church of God	Anderson	www.anderson.edu
Grace College and Seminary	1500	Fellowship of Grace Brethren Churches	Winona Lake	www.grace.edu
Goshen College	1000	The Mennonite Church	Goshen	www.goshen.edu
Bethel College	2000	The Missionary Church	Mishawaka	www.bethel-college.edu
Taylor University	2000	Nondenominational	Upland	www.taylor.edu
Huntington University	1300	Church of the United Brethren in Christ	Huntington	www.huntington.edu
Indiana Wesleyan University	15,400	The Wesleyan Church	Marion	www.indwes.edu

* Enrollment figures are as of Spring, 2010. They are derived from each institution's own reporting on its website. In nearly every case they represent total enrollment, which is higher than FTE.

A hypothetical Indiana Christian University could take advantage of these seven existing campuses (and various off-site classroom locations) in a number of ways. First, it could validate and promote its multiple faith heritages by creating on each campus a center for the study of a particular denominational heritage. (Taylor University, a nondenominational institution, could host a center for nonaligned Protestantism.) Thus the "heritage constituency" of each current school could be appeased while simultaneously encouraged to engage in an act of great collaboration (thus illustrating the idea that "identity" need not result in "exclusion").

Each residential student could be encouraged or required to choose one such heritage as a context for study for a semester or more. Rather than "losing" their school to a larger, interdenominational university, the respective denominations and judicatories could choose to see the advantage of introducing their history, values, ministries, and distinctives to a much larger constituency. This would be good for the churches as well, as they will welcome into their ranks emerging leaders who have a denominational commitment that is coupled with a broader exposure to the varieties of Christianity than one would encounter at a purely denominational institution.

Second, ICU could utilize the existing academic strengths of each of its component schools and campuses in order to diversify its identity and programs. The international service-learning program at Goshen, the Science Center at Huntington, the adult and professional studies program at Indiana Wesleyan—these are examples (among others) of unique contributions that these current institutions could bring to a merged ICU. A student living in the northern edge of Indiana—or a student drawn by the peace and justice motif at Goshen—could complete one's general education requirements there and then move or commute to Huntington for a first-rate science education (which could become the hallmark of the Huntington campus). Likewise, the ACCEL program for adult professional studies at Huntington could merge with the much larger program created by Indiana Wesleyan and direct its energies elsewhere, knowing that those tuition dollars would still be available to the larger university.

This example illustrates how ICU could realize some efficiencies by merging these institutions. While the current campuses would likely be maintained for another generation, over time there would have to be strategic decisions to invest more heavily in the physical facilities of one location than in another, or perhaps to not invest further in capital improvements at any campus but to move gradually toward the creation of a new central campus. One can imagine eventually a large, unified campus for residential students supported by dozens or more of small satellite locations through-out the state of Indiana and around the world. This would result in a configuration that is simultaneously local and global ("glocal") and simultaneously centralized and decentralized.

Likewise, while ICU in its early years would be likely to maintain the historic undergraduate core at each current campus, over time it would move toward a common core for traditional residential students supplemented by a plethora of specialized pro-gram offerings, most offered solely on one of the seven campuses or one or more of the satellite locations. This merger of programs would permit the merger of academic departments and the shar-ing of faculty and financial resources. It should also be noted that foundations and government funding agencies are typically more hospitable to programs that have potential for a broader (as op-posed or narrower) audience or constituency. Seven small student development offices would be less likely to attract notice for their grant requests, for instance, than one office that serves the entire population of the seven.

Finally, a merger of administrative units would result in fi-nancial efficiencies (via merger of public relations, development, planning, marketing, recruiting, registration, financial aid, student accounts, and presidential offices, etc.), even while recognizing the need for an ongoing administrative unit on each of the campuses.[26] Most importantly, these institutions would cease competing with each other for the same pool of students and faculty and instead direct those energies toward the creation of collaborative learning environments. This is not to eschew the value of competition in the pursuit of excellence; it is, however, to argue that if such com-petitive impulses were directed inward (e.g., program to program) rather than outward (school to school), the costs to the Kingdom of God would be smaller and the benefits at least as large.

26. Penn State University names a "Campus Executive Officer" (CEO) for each of its satellite campuses but has only one president, who serves from the main campus at State College.

These environments would be good for students as well. Indiana Christian University could allow an undergraduate student, for instance, to complete a major at one campus and general education courses at another, explore a faith heritage at a third, pursue graduate studies at a third, participate in athletic activities at a fourth, and perhaps study and service abroad in a fifth location, all the while earning credits toward a degree granted by a single institution (ICU). Using and expanding upon Indiana Wesleyan's network of classroom locations in churches and boardrooms across northeastern Indiana, many of these locations could be in the student's backyard. Aggressive growth of online programs would extend ICU's reach far beyond the state of Indiana. In short, the program offerings for the student would be greater, the odds of being able to access those offerings close to home would be higher, and the opportunities for diverse learning environments would be enhanced.

One particular strength that Indiana Christian University could actualize would be the development of a first-rate theological school through a merger of the existing bodies. Each of these universities is in some way publicly evangelical and each sponsors some sort of theological program at the undergraduate and/or graduate level. (For instance, Grace has a full, nationally respected seminary, Anderson a School of Theology, and Huntington a graduate program in Christian Ministries.) The merger of these faculty, students, and resources into a single, comprehensive entity (perhaps rooted at one particular location) would permit opportunities for cross-denominational ministry training, for the creation of specialized academic programs and tracks, and for serious academic research on the theological disciplines (something with which evangelical institutions are not often credited by their non-evangelical colleagues). The denominations with which these several institutions are affiliated together represent a tremendous resource for research on the multiple expression of the evangelical movement, among other things. The fact that they represent different theological traditions would only add to the strength of a combined effort.

There would be many challenges, of course, to the creation of something like Indiana Christian University. Will the sponsoring denominations truly release ownership (and control) of the institutions they have founded, invested in, and nurtured for so many years in order to create what will almost assuredly be viewed (hopefully wrongly) as a "least common denominator" institution? The logistics of merging the programs of seven institutions, much less seven campuses, would be overwhelming and may offset the financial advantages for a number of years. Although they would be attracted to the idea of larger, better-funded departments, faculty would likely struggle with the proposal that their programs and offices be moved to other campuses. And while the campuses are within the same state, that fact should not imply that there is necessarily an easy commute between them (true in some cases but not in others), which will make some of the location-specific program offerings daunting for the commuting student.

Nevertheless, if Indiana Christian University (or something like it) does not become reality, there will likely be other Christian universities that will explore other forms of merger or collaboration in the decades ahead (although most without the particular geographical advantage enjoyed by seven institutions within a particular portion of a single state). I have wondered aloud with administrators of both institutions whether Eastern University and Messiah College (located within 100 miles of each other in eastern Pennsylvania) should share a graduate school. Or—a more far-fetched idea—whether Eastern University and George Fox University should partner together to link East Coast to West Coast as two institutions with much in common: similar heritages of progressive, peace-and-justice evangelicalism; similar student enrollments (3500-4000); similar structures (a residential undergraduate college, graduate offerings, a somewhat loosely connected seminary, and off-campus classroom sites); and similar commitments to entrepreneurship and collaboration.

One suspects that by the middle of the twenty-first century, whether through efforts like those described above or initiatives yet unimagined, the landscape of Christian higher education in the United States will be dramatically different than it is at the beginning of the century. The question is whether it will be better. The study is intended to provide optimism that it can and will be so.

THE WAY OF COLLABORATION:
STRANGERS OR FELLOW PILGRIMS

Tim Herndon and Barbara Fredericks, whose fictional story opened this discussion in chapter 1, are both working from outdated assumptions about the relationship between church and academy—assumptions that were valid for the late twentieth century but increasingly suspect in the twenty-first. Yes, Western Christian University and its sponsoring denomination may never have the same relationship they enjoyed when Tim was an undergraduate student and, yes, there will continue to be tense discussions and debates about how widely or narrowly a university may cast its nets in the pursuit of truth (and in pursuit of those who specialize in seeking it). But there are awaiting them opportunities for a collaborative relationship that would serve both of them—and the constituencies they represent—very well.

They do, however, need to take some time to talk with each other, to re-imagine the relationship, and to think creatively about the future. The transformation awaiting them will have implications for how they teach students, serve congregations, and change their world. But this transformation cannot be accomplished by strangers. It can, however, be realized by fellow pilgrims who find themselves on the same journey and are willing to engage each other in dialogue about the risks and benefits of walking a new road together.

Bibliography

Adams, Charles C. "Technology from a Christian Perspective: An Evaluation of Albert Borgmann's 'Power Failure' and Egbert Schuurman's 'Faith and hope in Technology'—A Review Essay." *Christian Scholars Review* 33 (2004) 569–79.

Adams, James Luther. *Voluntary Associations: Socio-Cultural Analyses and Theological Interpretation.* Chicago: Exploration, 1988.

Anderson, Leith. *A Church for the Twenty-First Century.* Minneapolis: Bethany House, 1992.

———. *Dying for Change.* Minneapolis: Bethany House, 1998.

Ashkenas, Ron, Dave Ulrich, Todd Jick, and Steve Kerr. *The Boundaryless Organization: Breaking the Chains of Organization Structure.* Rev. ed. The Jossey-Bass Business and Management Series. San Francisco: Jossey-Bass, 2002.

Augustine, *Confessions.* Translated and edited by Henry Chadwick. New York: Oxford University Press, 1991.

Ayers, Steve. *Igniting Passion in Your Church: Becoming Intimate with Christ.* Loveland, CO: Group, 2002.

Baltzell, E. Digby. *Puritan Boston and Quaker Philadelphia.* Reprint ed. Piscataway, NJ: Transaction, 1996.

Banks, Robert. *Reenvisioning Theological Education: Exploring a Missional Alternative to Current Models.* Grand Rapids: Eerdmans, 1999.

Barna, George. *The Second Coming of the Church.* Nashville: Word, 1998.

Barton, Bruce. *The Man Nobody Knows: A Discovery of the Real Jesus.* Indianapolis: Bobbs-Merrill, 1925.

Baumgartner, Lisa M. "Self-directed Learning: A Goal, Process, and Personal Attribute." In *Adult Learning Theory: A Primer,* edited by Lisa M. Baumgartner et al., 23–28. Information Series (ERIC Clearinghouse on Adult, Career, and Vocational Education) 392. Columbus, OH: Center on Education and Training for Employment, College of Education, the Ohio State University, 2003.

Benjamin, R. "The Environment of Higher Education: A Constellation of Changes." *Annals of the American Academy of Political and Social Science* 585 (2003) 8–30.

Benne, Robert. *Quality with Soul: How Six Premier Colleges and Universities Keep Faith with Their Religious Traditions.* Grand Rapids: Eerdmans, 2001.

Berrigan, Daniel. *The Bride: Images of the Church.* Maryknoll, NY: Orbis, 2000.

Bickers, Dennis W. *The Tentmaking Pastor.* Grand Rapids: Baker, 2000.

Birden, S. "Critical and Postmodern Challenges for Education." In *Adult Learning Theory: A Primer,* edited by Lisa M. Baumgartner et al., 29–33. Information Series (ERIC Clearinghouse on Adult, Career, and Vocational Education) 392. Columbus, OH: Center on Education and Training for Employment, College of Education, the Ohio State University, 2003.

Blair, Anthony L. "Best Practices: Open Source Curriculum." *Journal of Continuing Higher Education* 54 (2006) 28–33.

—————. "Scattered and Divided: Itinerancy, Ecclesiology, and Revivalism in the Presbyterian Awakening." *Journal of Presbyterian History.* 81 (2003) 25–44.

—————. "The Original Spirit in Twenty-First Century Clothes." Unpublished paper presented at the United Brethren National Board Meeting, Huntington, Indiana, 14 February 2005.

Bok, Derek Curtis. *Universities in the Marketplace: The Commercialization of Higher Education.* Princeton: Princeton University Press, 2003.

Buber, Martin. *I and Thou.* Translated by Ronald Gregor Smith. New York: Scribners, 1937.

Buckley, William F., Jr. *God and Man at Yale: The Superstitions of "Academic Freedom."* Chicago: Regnery, 1951

Burtchaell, James Tunstead. "The Decline and Fall of the Christian College." *First Things* 12 (1991) 16–29.

—————. "The Decline and Fall of the Christian College (II)." *First Things* 13 (1991) 30–38.

—————. *The Dying of the Light: The Disengagement of Colleges and Universities from Their Christian Churches.* Grand Rapids: Eerdmans, 1998.

Butler, Joseph. *The Analogy of Religion, Natural and Revealed, to the Constitution and Course of Nature.* London, 1736.

Bynum, Caroline Walker. *Holy Feast, Holy Fast: The Religious Significance of Food to Medieval Women.* Berkeley: University of California Press, 1988.

Caroselli, Susanna Bede. "Instinctive Response as a Tool for the Scholar." In *Scholarship and Christian Faith: Enlarging the Conversation,* edited by Douglas G. Jacobsen and Rhonda Hustedt Jacobsen, 135–50. New York: Oxford, 2004.

Carroll, Colleen. *The New Faithful: Why Young Adults are Embracing Christian Orthodoxy.* Chicago: Loyola, 2002.

Cuninggim, Merrimon. *Uneasy Partners: The College and the Church*. Nashville: Abingdon, 1994.

Davis, Edward B. "Is There a Christian History of Science?" *Scholarship and Christian Faith: Enlarging the Conversation*, edited by Douglas G. Jacobsen and Rhonda Hustedt Jacobsen, 63–76. New York: Oxford, 2004.

Derrida, Jacques. *A Derrida Reader: Between the Blinds*. Edited by Peggy Kanuf. New York: Columbia University Press, 1991.

Dewey, John. *Experience and Education*. Reprint edition. New York: Free Press, 2007.

Discipline of the Church of the United Brethren in Christ USA. Huntington, IN: Department of Church Services, 2001.

Downing, Crystal. "Imbricating Faith and Learning: The Architectonics of Christian Scholarship." *Scholarship and Christian Faith: Enlarging the Conversation*, edited by Douglas G. Jacobsen and Rhonda Hustedt Jacobsen 33–44. New York: Oxford, 2004.

Easum, William M., and Dave Travis. *Beyond the Box: Innovative Churches That Work*. Loveland, CO: Group, 2003.

Escobar, Samuel. *The New Global Mission: The Gospel from Everywhere to Everyone*. Downers Grove, IL: InterVarsity, 2003.

Fein, A. D., and Logan, M. C. "Preparing Instructors for Online Instruction." *New Directions forAdult and Continuing Education* 100 (2003) 45–55.

Femia, Joseph V. *Gramsci's Political Thought: Hegemony, Consciousness, and the Revolutionary Consciousness*. New York: Clarendon, 1981.

Fidler, Dorothy S. "Teaching Adult Students." Lefton Learning Community. No pages. Online: http://www.abacon.com/lefton/adult.html.

Finney, Charles. *Lectures on Revival*. Minneapolis: Bethany House, 1989.

Finnis, John. *Moral Absolutes: Tradition, Revision, and Truth*. The Michael J. McGivney Lectures of the John Paul II Institute for Studies on Marriage and Family, 1988. Washington, DC: Catholic University of America Press, 1991.

————. "Secularism, Law, and Public Policy." Unpublished paper presented at "Faith and the Challenges of Secularism," Princeton University, Princeton, New Jersey, 10 October 2003.

Fitts, Robert, Sr. *The Church in the House: A Return to Simplicity*. Salem, OR: Preparing the Way, 2001.

Forgacs, David, editor. *The Antonio Gramsci Reader: Selected Writings, 1916–1935*. Edited by David Forgasc. New York: New York University Press, 2000.

Frost, Michael, and Alan Hirsch. *The Shaping of Things to Come: Innovation and Mission for the 21st-Century Church*. Peabody, MA: Hendrickson, 2003.

Fungaroli, Carole S. *Traditional Degrees for Nontraditional Students: How to Earn a Top Diploma from America's Great Colleges at Any Age*. New York: Farrar, Straus, and Giroux, 2000.

Gagne, Robert M., et al. *Principles of Instructional Design*. 5th ed. Belmont, CA: Wadsworth, 2004.

Gardner, Howard. *Changing Minds: The Art and Science of Changing Our Own and Other People's Minds*. Boston: Harvard Business School Press, 2004.

Gibbs, Eddie. *ChurchNext: Quantum Changes in How We Do Ministry*. Downers Grove, IL: InterVarsity, 2000.

Girard, René. *Things Hidden Since the Beginning of the World*. Translated by Michael Metteer and Stephen Bann. Stanford: Stanford University, 1987.

Gladwell, Malcolm. *The Tipping Point: How Little Things Can Make a Big Difference*. Boston: Back Bay, 2002.

Godin, Seth. *Purple Cow: Transform Your Business by Being Remarkable*. New York: Portfolio, 2003.

———. *Unleashing the Ideavirus*. New York: Hyperion, 2001.

Goldstein, Niles Elliot. *God at the Edge: Searching for the Divine in Uncomfortable and Unexpected Places*. New York: Bell Tower, 2000.

Grove, David J., and Basil Panzer. *Resolving Traumatic Memories: Metaphors and Symbols in Psychotherapy*. New York: Irvington, 1989.

Hall, Douglas John. *The Cross in our Context: Jesus and the Suffering World*. Minneapolis: Fortress, 2003.

Hambrick-Stowe, Charles E. *Charles G. Finney and the Spirit of American Evangelicalism*. Library of Religious Biography. Grand Rapids: Eerdmans, 1996.

Hamilton, Michael, and James Mathisen. "Faith and Learning at Wheaton College." In *Models for Christian Higher Education: Strategies for Success in the Twenty-First Century*, edited by Richard T. Hughes and William B. Adrian, 261–83. Grand Rapids: Eerdmans, 1997.

Hanna, Donald E. *Higher Education in an Era of Digital Competition: Choices and Challenges*. Madison, WI: Atwood, 2000.

Harries, Richard. *God Outside the Box: Why Spiritual People Object to Christianity*. London: SPCK, 2002.

Hersh, Richard H., and John Merrow, editors. *Declining By Degrees: Higher Education at Risk*. New York: Palgrave Macmillan, 2005.

Hiebert, Paul G., and Eloise Hiebert Meneses. *Incarnational Ministry: Planting Churches in Band, Tribal, Peasant, and Urban Societies*. Grand Rapids: Baker, 1995.

Hirsch, E. D., Jr., Joseph F. Kett, and James S. Trefil, editors. *The New Dictionary of Cultural Literacy*, 3rd ed. Boston: Houghton Mifflin, 2002.

Holmes, Arthur Frank. *All Truth is God's Truth*. Downers Grove, IL: InterVarsity, 1977.

———. *The Idea of a Christian College*. Grand Rapids: Eerdmans, 1975.

Hope, Jane. "Editorial: Web Accessibility in Higher Education." *Interactions* 5:3 (2001) no pages. Online: http://www2.warwick.ac.uk/services/ldc/resource/interactions/archive/issue15.

Hueth, Alan C. "E-Learning and Christian Higher Education: War of the Worlds or Lessons in Reductionism?" *Christian Scholars Review* 33 (2004) 529.

Hughes, Richard T., and William B. Adrian, editors. *Models for Christian Higher Education: Strategies for Success in the Twenty-First Century*. Grand Rapids: Eerdmans, 1997.

Huntington, Samuel P. *The Clash of Civilizations and the Remaking of World Order*. New York: Simon & Schuster, 1998.

Jacobsen, Douglas, and Rhonda Hustedt Jacobsen. *Scholarship and Christian Faith: Enlarging the Conversation*. New York: Oxford, 2004.

Jenkins, Philip. *The Next Christendom: The Coming of Global Christianity*. New York: Oxford, 2003.

John of the Cross. *The Dark Night of the Soul*. Translated and edited by Mirabai Starr. New York: Penguin Putnam, 2002.

Johnson, Phillip E. *The Wedge of Truth: Splitting the Foundations of Naturalism*. Downers Grove, IL: InterVarsity, 2000.

Johnson, S. D., and Aragon, S. R. "An Instructional Strategy Framework for Online Learning Environments." *New Directions for Adult and Continuing Education* 100 (2003) 31–43.

Jones, Laurie Beth. *Jesus CEO: Using Ancient Wisdom for Visionary Leadership*. New York: Hyperion, 1995.

Julian of Norwich. *The Wisdom of Julian of Norwich*. Compiled and introduced by Monica Furlong. Grand Rapids: Eerdmans, 1997.

Kant, Immanuel. *Groundwork of the Metaphysics of Morals*. Edited by Mary J. Gregor. Cambridge Texts in the History of Philosophy. Cambridge: Cambridge University Press, 1998.

Keizer, Garrett. "Career Ministry: Two Cheers for Professional Clergy." *The Christian Century* 119:9 (2002) 30–33.

Keller, George. *Academic Strategy: The Management Revolution in American Higher Education*. Baltimore: Johns Hopkins, 1983.

———. *Transforming a College: The Story of a Little-Known College's Strategic Climb to National Distinction*. Baltimore: Johns Hopkins, 2004.

Klinghoffer, David. *The Lord Will Gather Me In: My Journey to Jewish Orthodoxy*. New York: Free Press, 2002.

Knowles, Malcolm S. *The Modern Practice of Adult Education: From Pedagogy to Andragogy*. Rev. ed. Chicago: Follett, 1980.

———. *The Adult Learner: A Neglected Species*. Building Blocks of Human Potential Series. Houston: Gulf, 1973.

Kolb, David. *Experiential Learning: Experience as the Source of Learning and Development*. Upper Saddle River, NJ: Prentice Hall, 1984.

Kostner, Jaclyn. *Virtual Leadership: Secrets from the Round Table for the Multi-Site Manager*. New York: Warner, 1994.

Kreider, Larry, and C. Peter Wagner. *House Church Networks: A Church for a New Generation*. Ephrata, PA: House to House, 2002.

Kreider, Larry, et al. *New House Church Networks*. Audio recording. Ephrata, PA: House to House, n.d..

Kurth, James. "Clash of Worldviews." Unpublished paper presented at "Faith and the Challenges of Secularism," Princeton University, Princeton, New Jersey, 10 October 2003.

Lakoff, George, and Mark Turner. *More Than Cool Reason: A Field Guide to Poetic Metaphor*. Chicago: University of Chicago Press, 1989.

Lawley, James, and Penny Tompkins. *Metaphors in Mind: Transformation through Symbolic Modelling*. London: Developing Company, 2000.

Lesser, Eric L., Michael A. Fontaine, and Jason A. Slusher, editors. *Knowledge and Communities*. Resources for the Knowledge-Based Economy Series. Boston: Butterworth-Heineman, 2000.

Lewis, Bernard. *What Went Wrong? The Clash Between Islam and Modernity in the Middle East*. New York: Perennial, 2003.

Locke, John. *An Essay Concerning Human Understanding*. New York: Dover, 1959.

Longenecker, Richard, N., editor. *Community Formation in the Early Church and in the Church Today*. Peabody, MA: Hendrickson, 2002.

MacGavran, Donald A., and C. Peter Wagner. *Understanding Church Growth*. 3rd ed. Grand Rapids: Eerdmans, 1990.

MacIntyre, Alasdair. *Whose Justice? Which Rationality?* South Bend, IN: University of Notre Dame Press, 1988.

Manning, Brennan. *Ruthless Trust: The Ragamuffin's Path to God*. San Francisco: HarperCollins, 2000.

Marsden, George M. *The Outrageous Idea of Christian Scholarship*. New York: Oxford University Press, 1997.

———. *The Soul of the American University: From Protestant Establishment to Established Nonbelief*. New York: Oxford University Press, 1994.

———. "The Soul of the American University." *First Things* (January, 1991) 34–47.

Marsden, George M., and Brad Longfield, editors. *The Secularization of the Academy*. Religion in America Series. New York: Oxford University Press, 1992.

Marti, Gerardo. *A Mosaic of Believers: Diversity and Innovation in a Multiethnic Church*. Bloomington: Indiana University Press, 2005.

McLaren, Brian D. *A Generous Orthodoxy: Why I am a Missional, Evangelical, Post/Protestant Liberal/Conservative, Mystical/Poetic, Biblical, Charismatic/ Contemplative, Fundamentalist/Calvinist, Anabaptist/Anglican, Methodist, Catholic, Green, Incarnational, Depressed-yet-Hopeful, Emergent, Unfinished Christian*. Grand Rapids: Zondervan, 2004.

———. *More Ready Than You Realize: Evangelism as Dance in the Postmodern Matrix*. Grand Rapids: Zondervan, 2002.

————. *A New Kind of Christian: A Tale of Two Friends on a Spiritual Journey.* San Francisco: Jossey-Bass, 2001.

Mead, Frank Spencer, and Samuel S. Hill. *Handbook of Denominations in the United States.* 11th ed. Revised by Craig D. Atwood. Nashville: Abingdon, 2001.

Morgan, Edmund S. *Visible Saints: The History of a Puritan Idea.* Ithaca, NY: Cornell University Press, 1965. First published 1963 by New York University Press.

Murphy, Mark C., editor. *Alasdair MacIntyre.* Contemporary Philosophy in Focus. Cambridge: Cambridge University Press, 2003.

Naugle, David. "The Christian College and Adult Education." *Faculty Dialogue* 24 (1995) 24–27.

Neighbour, Ralph W. *Where Do We Go From Here? A Guidebook for the Cell Group Church.* Rev. ed. Houston: Touch Outreach Ministries, 2000.

Neuhaus, Richard John. *The Naked Public Square: Religion and Democracy in America.* 2nd ed. Grand Rapids: Eerdmans, 1996.

————. "Secularism, Law, and Public Policy." Unpublished paper presented at "Faith and the Challenges of Secularism," Princeton University, Princeton, New Jersey, 11 October 2003.

Newman, John Henry, et al. *The Idea of a University.* Edited by Frank M. Turner. Rethinking the Western Tradition. New Haven, CT: Yale University Press, 1996.

Niebuhr, H. Richard. *Christ and Culture.* Harper Torchbooks. San Francisco: Harper & Row, 1975.

Nielsen, Donald A. "Troeltsch, Ernst." In *Encyclopedia of Religion and Society,* edited by William H. Swatos. Walnut Creek, CA: Altamira Press, 1998. Online: http://hirr.hartsem.edu/ency/Troeltsch.htm.

Noll, Mark A. *The Scandal of the Evangelical Mind.* Grand Rapids: Eerdmans, 1995.

Oden, Thomas C. *Requiem: A Lament in Three Movements.* Nashville: Abingdon, 1995.

Oh, C. H. "Information Communication Technology and the New University: A View on E-learning." *Annals of the American Academy of Political and Social Science* 585 (2003) 134–53.

Paley, William. *Natural Theology; or Evidences of the Existence and Attributes of the Deity.* London: Faulder, 1802.

Palloff, Rena M., and Keith Pratt. *The Virtual Student: A Profile and Guide to Working With Online Learners.* The Jossey-Bass Higher and Adult Education Series. San Francisco: Jossey-Bass, 2003.

Perkins, Spencer, and Chris Rice. *More Than Equals: Racial Healing for the Sake of the Gospel.* Downers Grove, IL: InterVarsity, 2000.

Piper, John. *Brothers, We Are Not Professionals: A Plea to Pastors for Radical Ministry.* Nashville: Broadman & Holman, 2002.

Platinga, Alvin. "Science and Secularism." Unpublished paper presented at "Faith and the Challenges of Secularism," Princeton University, Princeton, New Jersey, 10 October 2003.

Plato. *Apology, Crito, Phaedo, Symposium, Republic.* Translated by B. Jowett. Edited by Louise Ropes Loomis. Toronto: Van Nostrand, 1942.

Polanyi, Michael. *Personal Knowledge: Toward a Post-Critical Philosophy.* New York: Harper and Row, 1962.

Rhodes, Stephen A. *Where the Nations Meet: The Church in a Multicultural World.* Downers Grove, IL: InterVarsity, 1998.

Richards, Lawrence O. *A Theology of Christian Education.* Grand Rapids: Zondervan, 1980.

Richards, Lawrence O., and Clyde Hoeldtke, *A Theology of Church Leadership.* Grand Rapids: Zondervan, 1980.

Riddell, Mike, Cathy Kirkpatrick, and Mark Pierson. *The Prodigal Project: Journey Into the Emerging Church.* London: SPCK, 2000.

Roels, Shirley J. "Global Discipleship and Online Learning: What Does Blackboard Have to do With Jerusalem?" *Christian Scholars Review* 33 (2004) 461.

Roy, Olivier. *Globalised Islam: The Search for a New Ummah.* New York: Columbia University Press, 2004.

Sanders, John. *The God Who Risks: A Theology of Providence.* Downers Grove, IL: InterVarsity, 1998.

Sanders, John, and Christopher A. Hall. "Does God Know Your Next Move? Part One." *Christianity Today* 45:7 (2001) 38–45.

———. "Does God Know Your Next Move? Part Two." *Christianity Today* 45:8 (2001) 50–56.

Sartre, Jean-Paul Sartre. *Existentialism and Humanism.* Translate by Philip Mairet. London: Metheun, 1948.

Sawatsky, Rodney J. "The Virtue of Scholarly Hope." In *Scholarship and Christian Faith: Enlarging the Conversation,* edited by Douglas G. Jacobsen and Rhonda Hustedt Jacobsen, 3–14. New York: Oxford University Press, 2004.

Schaller, Lyle E. *The Small Church is Different.* Nashville: Abingdon, 1982.

———. *The Very Large Church.* Nashville: Abingdon, 2000.

Schultz, Howard, and Dori Jones Yang. *Pour Your Heart Into It: How Starbucks Built a Company One Cup at a Time.* New York: Hyperion, 1997.

Schwarz, Christian. *Natural Church Development: A Guide to Eight Essential Qualities of Healthy Churches.* 3rd ed. Carol Stream, IL: ChurchSmart, 1996.

Schweitzer, Albert. *The Quest of the Historical Jesus.* Edited by John Bowden. Minneapolis: Fortress, 2001.

Scott, P. A. "Attributes of High-Quality Intensive Courses." *New Directions for Adult and Continuing Education* 97 (2003) 29–38.

Scruton, Roger. "Clash of Worldviews." Unpublished paper presented at "Faith and the Challenges of Secularism," Princeton University, Princeton, New Jersey, 10 October 2003.

———. *The Meaning of Conservatism*. Rev. 3rd ed. South Bend, IN: St. Augustine's, 2002.

Senge, Peter M. *The Fifth Discipline: The Art and Practice of the Learning Organization*. New York: Currency, 1990.

Sennett, James F., editor. *The Analytic Theist: An Alvin Plantinga Reader*. Grand Rapids: Eerdmans, 1998.

Simson, Wolfgang. *Houses That Change the World*. Waynesboro, GA: OM Publishing, 2001.

Slater, Robert Slater. *The Wal-Mart Decade: How a New Generation of Leaders Turned Sam Walton's Legacy into the World's #1 Company*. New York: Portfolio, 2003.

Slaughter, Michael, with Warren Bird. *Unlearning Church: Just When You Had Leadership All Figured Out*. Loveland, CO: Group, 2002.

Smith, Adam. *The Wealth of Nations*. Edited by Edwin Cannan. New York: Modern Library, 1994.

Smith, David L. "Technology and Pedagogical Meaning: Lessons from the Language Classroom." *Christian Scholars Review* 33 (2004) 511.

Spader, Dann, and Gary Mayes. *Growing a Healthy Church: The SonLife Strategy*. Chicago: Moody, 1991.

Stanley, Andy. *The Next Generation Leader: Five Essentials for Those Who Will Shape the Future*. Sisters, OR: Multnomah, 2003.

Steck, H. "Corporatization of the University: Seeking Conceptual Clarity." *Annals of the American Academy of Political and Social Science* 585 (2003) 66–83.

Stockstill, Larry. *The Cell Church: Preparing Your Church for the Coming Harvest*. Ventura, CA: Regal, 1998.

Stuhlman, Daniel D. "Knowledge Management Terms." Stuhlman Management Consultants. No pages. Online: http://home.earthlink.net/~ddstuhlman/defin1.htm.

Sweet, Leonard, editor. *Church in Emerging Culture: Five Perspectives*. Grand Rapids: Zondervan, 2003.

Sweet, Leonard. *A Cup of Coffee at the Soul Café*. Nashville: Broadman and Holman, 1998.

———. *Jesus Drives Me Crazy*. Grand Rapids: Zondervan, 2003.

———. *Out of the Question . . . Into the Mystery: Getting Lost in the Godlife Relationship*. Colorado Springs: Waterbrook, 2004.

———. *Post–modern Pilgrims: First Century Passion for the Twenty-First Century World*. Nashville: Broadman and Holman, 2000.

———. *Soul Tsunami: Sink or Swim in the New Millennium Culture*. Grand Rapids: Zondervan, 1999.

Teresa of Avila, *The Interior Castle*. Translated by E. Allison Peers. Garden City, NY: Image, 1972.

Tinknor, Raymond L. *Help Stamp Out Biblical Illiteracy*. Winona Lake, IN: Institute for Biblical Renewal, 1980.

Tomlinson, Dave. *The Post Evangelical*. Grand Rapids: Zondervan, 2003.

Towns, Elmer, and Warren Bird. *Into the Future: Turning Today's Church Trends into Tomorrow's Opportunities*. Grand Rapids: Revell, 2000.

Troeltsch, Ernst. *The Social Teaching of the Christian Churches*. Translated by Olive Wyon. Library of Theological Ethics. Louisville: Westminster John Knox, 1992.

Volf, Miroslav. *After Our Likeness: The Church as the Image of the Trinity*. Grand Rapids: Eerdmans, 1998.

Wachs, Martin. *The Case for Practitioner Faculty*. Los Angeles: Graduate School of Architecture and Urban Planning, University of California, Los Angeles,1993.

Webber, Robert. *Ancient-Future Faith: Rethinking Evangelicalism for a Postmodern World*. Grand Rapids: Baker, 1999.

Weigel, Van B.. *Deep Learning for a Digital Age: Technology's Untapped Potential to Enrich Higher Education*. The Jossey-Bass Higher and Adult Education Series. San Francisco: Jossey-Bass, 2002.

Weinberger, Marvin I. "Just in Time Learning." *Library Trends* 45 (1997) 623.

Wenger, Etienne. *Communities of Practice: Learning, Meaning, and Identity*. Cambridge: Cambridge University Press, 1999.

Westerkamp, Marilyn. *Triumph of the Laity: Scots-Irish Piety and the Great Awakening, 1625–1760*. New York: Oxford, 1988.

Willard, Dallas. *The Divine Conspiracy: Rediscovering our Hidden Life in God*. San Francisco: HarperCollins, 1998.

———. *Renovation of the Heart: Putting on the Character of Christ*. Colorado Springs: NavPress, 2002.

Willmer, Wesley K., and J. David Schmidt. *The Prospering Parachurch: Enlarging the Boundaries of God's Work*. New York: Jossey-Bass, 1998.

Wlodkowski, R. J., and C. E. Kasworm. "Accelerated Learning: Future Roles and Influences." *New Directions for Adult and Continuing Education* 97 (2003) 93–97.

Wolfe, Alan. *The Transformation of American Religion: How We Actually Live Our Faith*. New York: Free Press, 2003.

Wolterstorff, Nicholas. *Reason within the Bounds of Religion*. Grand Rapids: Eerdmans, 1976.

Yancey, George. *One Body, One Spirit: Principles of Successful Multiracial Churches*. Downers Grove, IL: InterVarsity, 2003.

Index

A

accelerated programs, 69, 75
adjunct instructors, 70, 71, 72
Adrian, William, 55, 56, 64, 84
adult education, 66, 68, 70, 82
adult students, 11, 65, 66, 69, 71,
    75, 102
affinity group, 42
American Baptists, 9, 94
American Christianity, 17, 51
American Church, 16, 48
Anabaptist, 61, 89
Anderson University, 110, 114
andragogy, 67
Anglicans, 41
anti-intellectualism, 61
APEPT, 46
Apostle Paul, 45
Aristotle, 15, 22
asynchronous, 74
attractional model, 38, 39, 48, 93
Augustine, 26
autonomy, 25, 26, 27, 55, 60
Ayers, Stephen, 20
Azusa Pacific University, 52

B

Baker, Robin, viii, 99

Banks, Robert, 84, 96
Baptists, 40, 47
Beliot College, 52
Benedictines, 19
Benne, Robert, 56, 84
Berrigan, Daniel, 20
Bethel College, 86, 110
Bible Church, 40
Bible college, 2, 66
biblical illiteracy, 81
bivocational ministers, 45
Black, David, 92
Blackboard, 74, 103
Boehm, Martin, 89
Boston College, 52
Brandt, H. David, 99
Buckley, William, 51, 53
Burtchaell, James, 51, 52, 53, 54,
    55
Butler, Joseph, 56
Bynum, Caroline Walker, 20

C

California Lutheran University, 55
Calvary Chapel, 40
Calvin College, 55, 58
Campolo, Tony, 92, 98
Capella University, 102
Caroselli, Susanna Bede, 60